# Costume Jewelry
## The Great Pretenders

Lyngerda Kelley
Nancy Schiffer

Schiffer Publishing Ltd

West Chester, Pennsylvania 19380

# Acknowledgments

Many people have shared their time, knowledge, collections and good humor to bring this book into being. We publicly thank Claire Shepard at Asprey's, London; Marian R. Carroll, Dennis Cogdell, Frances Cronan and Frances Detweiler, Jackie Fleischmann, Aggie Moore, and Ronnie Seigle at the Black Angus Antique Mall, Adamstown, Pa.; Ann's Arts in Chestnut Hill, Pa.; Diana Foley at Gray's Mews, London; Maureen McEvoy and Linda Morgan at the Islington Antique Mall, London; Rebecca Frey, Joan Leibowitz, and Lorraine Matt at The Lafayette Mill Antique Center, Lafayette, N.J.; Matthew and Michael in Lahaska, Pa.; Kiki McDonough in London; Nora Lee at Bizarre Bazaar and Terry Rogers at The Manhattan Art and Antique Center, N.Y.C.; Norman Crider at Trump Tower; Bob Coyle and Marianne Ward, The Peoples' Store, Lambertville, N.J.; Mim Klein in Philadelphia; Miss Genevieve and Kenneth J. Lane of Kenneth J. Lane, Inc., Patricia Funt, Michael Greenberg, Muriel Karasik, Angela Kramer, and Carol Lupo at Trifari, N.Y. city; Karen Carmichael, Neal Davis, Matilda D. Knowles II, Judy Pyle, and Scott and Wendy Tyson. Each of them will recognize some old friends in the following pages and recall our dragging note pads, cameras, lights and questions into their spaces to gather our material and pictures. It has been an enjoyable and informative adventure for us; thank you for your important contributions. Your love of costume jewelry is infectious.

Copyright © 1987 by Lyngerda Kelley and Nancy Schiffer.
Library of Congress Catalog Number: 87-61432.

Printed in the United States of America.
ISBN: 0-88740-113-9
Published by Schiffer Publishing Ltd.
1469 Morstein Road, West Chester, Pennsylvania 19380

This book may be purchased from the publisher.
Please include $2.00 postage.
Try your bookstore first.

Title page:
Necklace with three red stones in cast metal setting. / Link bracelet and earrings with blue glass and rhinestones. / Earrings of gold colored metal, glass cabuchon and rhinestone. / Necklace of iridescent, blue and nugget glass stones, all by Schiaparelli, circa 1950. *Muriel Karasik.*

# Contents

# Costume Jewelry in History

The articles of costume jewelry presented in this book are generally a part of the jewelry styles derived from the European traditions of the nineteenth and twentieth centuries. While the term costume used in this context can refer specifically to inexpensive, mass produced imitations of fine jewelry and gems, this group goes well beyond mere imitations. The materials used initially to imitate were themselves explored and found able to produce effects quite different than any known styles. The early glass imitation gems were lighter weight than the gemstones they were designed to replicate. Therefore, much larger stones could be fabricated in glass than would be used for real jewelry. Therefore also quite different designs were possible for costume jewelry than were practical with gems. The same size gem stones would be prohibitively expensive for most people and sometimes the same settings would be impossible in the traditional materials. With advancements in technology came the ability to produce materials in large quantities for low cost.

Costume jewelry now is the ornamentation of the majority.

Imitations of expensive metalwork and gemstones have been used for personal adornment since far back in antiquity. As most artistic styles have spread to the Western world from the East, so did the knowledge of gems and jewelry. Diamonds originated first in India from where stories of their brilliance and hardness spread to Europe. Jewelry from the ancient civilizations in Egypt and Turkey are represented by fine metal work and strings of beads, bone, and shell, which can be viewed at art museums worldwide. Design, color sense and lapidary skills were already quite advanced.

Examples of early Greek, Chinese, Roman and European jewelry furnish prototypes for copies and new interpretations which make up the history of not only real but also of costume jewelry. A study of the development of jewelry styles can be a fascinating exercise which incorporates social, fashion and mineral history. An overview is presented in Hugh Tait's book *Seven Thousand Years of*

Two pins with silver backings and paste stones with silver foil backings, English, eighteenth century. Left with gold band engraved *Hoc Signo Vinces In Memento Mori.* Variously shaped stones and black pitch dots are evident in both examples. *Patricia Funt.*

Brooch of silver with foil backed paste, French, late eighteenth century in popular girandole design. *Michael Greenberg.*

*Jewellry*, based on the jewelry collections at the Victoria and Albert Museum in London. Other jewelry collections at, for example, the Metropolitan Museum of Art in New York, The Walters Art Gallery in Baltimore, and those at the major museums of the world will give a perspective of the developments in jewelry design in each region of the world that has contributed to the evolving styles.

Writing of Mediterranean glass in the periods from the fifteenth to first centuries B.C., W. B. Honey claims "glassmaking was still more or less tied to the imitation of precious stones and in tutelage to the art of the lapidary." (Glass, *Victoria and Albert Museum Handbook,* London, 1946, p.13) Medieval chemists tried countless ways to change ordinary metals into gold, and glassmakers of those days continued to create imitations of precious stones.

From about the ninth through fourteenth centuries, Venice was the center of glassmaking in Europe and Venetian colored glass gemstones were exported in large quantities to all parts of Europe (p.25 Lewis -*Paste*). Still, most jewelry made at this period had elaborate metalwork and used enamels for color. Cabochon gemstones were used primarily for their superstitious properties, not in jewelry. In fact, very little glass-set jewelry has survived from before the 18th century.

During the fifteenth and sixteenth centuries colored stones gradually were more important in jewelry design and European lapidaries learned to polish and facet diamonds to bring out the reflective properties unique to their structure. During the sixteenth century, diamonds were more frequently found mounted in jewelry which was worn primarily by wealthy men and for religious purposes. At this time, too, new diamond mines were opened at Golconda, India, so the diamond supply to Europe was greatly increased.

By the seventeenth century, France emerged as the artistic center of Europe and here jewelry designers emerged as a distinctive group. Rose-cut diamonds were more commonly featured in jewelry as enameled metal work took a more passive role in the designs. Wonderful Spanish and French pins from this period remain in significant numbers to be seen and compared. The typical style has three major gems set as drops from entwined metal ribbons.

In England a deposit of natural clear crystal was found near Bristol in the seventeenth century. When cut into rose-cut form for jewelry, these crystals were referred to as "Bristows" and were used as a type of imitation diamond.

Once again in England, the glass industry was significantly changed when, about 1675, quantities of lead oxide were added to the standard glass formula to produce flint glass—a truly clear material that was acclaimed throughout Europe for its ability to better imitate diamonds. Flint glass could be polished highly, unlike earlier glass, and had a very reflective effect. For centuries it had been known that foil backings on paste stones added significantly to the reflective properties of the glass, regardless of its cut facets. Yet the use of foils was not limited to glass, for before the early 18th century, diamonds and colored gems were often foiled to improve their color and reflectance. Settings were usually solid across the backs, and the space in which the stone fit was lined with a thin, highly polished sheet of reflective metal— either colored or silver. The colors of the foils added greatly to the resulting colors of otherwise dull stones. If no moisture seeps behind the stone to tarnish the foil, past stones should remain bright indefinitely.

Only at the end of the 17th century did a Venetian lapidary develop the "brilliant-cut" for diamonds with 58 facets. This new cut revealed the diamond's unique natural property to reflect light and sparkle without the need for foil backing.

During the 17th century, too, improved candles brought flickering artificial light indoors, and that enabled useful hours after dark to be productive. In candle light, jewelry set with reflective stones reflects an attractive and enticing quality which popularized the use of sparkling stones.

By the end of the seventeenth century, the combined knowledge of cutting gemstones, making clear glass, using improved foils to increase reflectance, and improved lighting made possible the popularity of good quality paste jewelry.

Along with interest in perfecting imitation stones, artificial gold was still the goal of many jewelers, as it had been since the Middle Ages. Christopher Pinchbeck (1670-1732), a watchmaker in London, invented in about 1720 an alloy of about 83% copper and 17% zinc to imitate gold for jewelry. Used mainly in watchmaking and chatelaines of the period, very few pieces remain of his original alloy. The French, however, used the principle he discovered extensively especially later in the eighteenth century, and in 1785 in Paris an alloy of copper with a thin coating of gold was invented (*Pomponne*) and used for jewelry. Items of copper and zinc alloy made in the nineteenth century include earrings and bracelets, and occasionally a necklace, usually of extremely fine quality. These are called Pinchbeck today, whether or not they are the same alloy Christopher Pinchbeck discovered.

By the mid-eighteenth century, European tastes in jewelry emphasized faceted diamonds. Portraits of wealthy men and increasingly more women of the day include extravagant amounts of lace, patterned brocades, gold work, gemstones and diamonds. As the middle classes were gradually rising throughout Europe, more interest in copying fancy gems in less expensive styles was developing.

In France, Georges-Frederic Strass (1701-1773), a German jeweler perfected a glass compound to imitate precious stones by 1735. These French pastes were immediately popular and resulted in the name Strass being ever-after associated with all imitation stones. Strass also was appointed Jeweler to the King of France in 1734, but this accomplishment did not alone insure his fame. The popularity of Strass's glass stones also invited imitators, and although there were manufacturers of counterfeit diamonds and other gems before Strass, by 1767 there were over 300 members of a "false jewelers" corporation (*bijoutiers-faussetiers*) in Paris alone. Their work is only mentioned in the context of loose stones; no reference is made directly to jewelry. (Lewis, *Paste*, p.38)

However, gradually imitation gems became readily available, and jewelry designers discovered that paste stones were soft enough to be cut into any desired size and shape. Settings could be made so that the stones fit tightly against each other, without spaces or metal work visible as is usually found with real gemstones. Designs for paste jewelry could be far more imaginative to include many more stones of larger sizes and various colors. The examples which remain from the period 1750-1850 present a wide and fascinating variety of styles which sometimes required more technical skill of the manufacturer than for settings of real gems. Upon initial inspection, the appearance of variously shaped stones in a setting can be the first clue to the use of imitation stones, whereas completely uniform and regular stones may be real gems.

An apparent means of attaching paste stones to their settings in the eighteenth century was the use of a small dot of black pitch at the base of the stone. Early examples of diamonds and colored gems also were sometimes set this way, but generally the resulting appearance of a black spot seen through its top identifies the stone as paste.

Besides diamonds and colored gems, glassmakers between 1780 and 1820 were able to imitate opals with a special form of glass known as 'opaline'. In this type of glass an overall white appearance with scattered particles reflects blue light, and with a rose-colored foil behind, the stone resembles true opal. Examples in the Victoria and Albert Museum in London are noteworthy.

In the nineteenth century jewelers were supported by a clientele that was growing ever more wealthy and socially competitive. Technology brought faster and advanced machinery to the manufacturing processes which resulted in larger volume and lower costs.

New diamond mines were opened in South Africa in the 1860's. The resulting flood of diamonds to Europe made them increasingly popular in jewelry. As the century progressed, settings were designed with prongs or with crimped (*mille-grain*) rims instead of solid rims as before. These new settings produced a gradual trend toward designs with increased open spaces around the stones.

The transition to the new open styles was not entirely successful with paste stones since they all had enclosed backs and metal rims. While colored stones, which relied on foils and tints for their appearance, continued in use in the old style settings, clear glass stones, which could not be polished as highly as true diamonds, gradually faded from popularity. Not until the techniques for making clear stones changed again did clear glass stones once more gain prominence in jewelry.

Advances in the glass industry in the 1840's included the use of various "silvering" processes to back mirrors. When this same process was applied to colorless glass jewelry stones successfully the use of foils gradually diminished. Permanently backed (silvered) stones now could be used in the new open-style settings.

Paintings of the English and French courts at the middle of the 19th century relate the taste for bangle bracelets and the absence of earrings. In England when Queen Victoria went into deep mourning for her husband, Prince Albert, in 1861, her countrymen and much of the English-speaking world joined her. Black jewelry became required at Victoria's court and was popular elsewhere. Therefore, a coal-derived stone called jet, mined at Whitby, England, was used to fashion jewelry until it became exhausted. Copies of jet jewelry in black glass, sometimes called French jet, became common and widespread.

In the mid-nineteenth century clothing and jewelry fashions were influenced by discoveries of ancient Roman sites at Pompeii and Herculaneum and of Etruscan tombs near Rome. Gold jewelry found here provoked a broad cry in Europe for reproductions with fine gold filigree wires and granulations. The resulting Classical style is called Archaeological and it includes, besides fine gold work, mounted Roman coins and fine mosaics. Revivals of these styles in costume jewelry have persisted to the middle of the twentieth century.

Another important nineteenth century style was the revival of Renaissance enamels and the use of cabochon stones set in gold. After U.S. Admiral Perry "opened" Japan, in 1863, Western artists were broadly influenced by Japanese designs. Presented to the West at the International Exhibitions at London in 1862, in Paris in 1867, and in Philadelphia in 1876, Japanese styles of naturalistic floral and bird designs influenced all of the western arts as well as jewelry. Ultimately, Art Nouveau styles of the early twentieth century stem in part from Japanese prototypes as they were interpreted by Western artists.

Each of the nineteenth century revival styles was produced in costume as well as real jewelry. Cameos were made in shell to replicate stone examples. More examples will be found in the groups of necklaces, bracelets, pins and earrings further along in this book.

By the late nineteenth century, women's clothing required a prescribed curved profile of high bust, small tapering long waist, and close fitting hips with full, long skirt.

Jewelry was designed to complement this style of clothing. Necklaces brought attention to the long line at the neck and upper chest. Choker styles were common and long beads were often worn in conjunction with chokers to accentuate the long waist line. Earrings were not spectacular affairs now, but added a small sparkle or color to the overall appearance. Hair styles were uniformly long strands piled high upon the head. For these, tiaras and hair pins and combs were popular for evening wear, and most were designed with diamonds. Imitation hair ornaments were also made in the diamond styles.

Jewelry in the first ten years of the new century followed the Art Nouveau styles of floral designs. Soft lines in ornamental design included frequent romantic use of idealized women and men embracing, with long flowing hair and extending tendrils in supra-naturalistic patterns; pastel-toned stones and glass techniques were explored to create new images.

In the first decade of the twentieth century clothing fashions evolved from the curving silhouette of the late nineteenth century to a classical pillar-like shape with a high waist popularly known as "Empire."

In England, Edward VIII's reign from 1901 to 1910 is characterized in jewelry design by the extended use of platinum as a new material for settings. Since new platinum mines were opened in Canada and South America, supplies to the West were abundant. Its strong and heavy properties made platinum's use as wires and prongs particularly appropriate for the more open settings that were being designed. In 1913, the first cultured pearls were released for sale, bringing the cost of this important fashion look into reach for a wider clientele.

The world suffered the bitterness of war between 1914 and 1917. Military efforts took precedence over high fashion and jewelry designs remained unchanged for the most part.

By 1917 skirts were dramatically shortened to about eight inches above the ground. Gradually, dress styles became more tubular with little or no

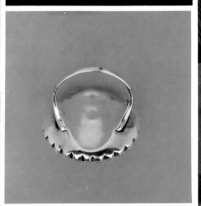

Ring of silver and paste, clear glass with silver foiled backs. French, c. 1795. *Kiki McDonough.*

Earrings of gold colored metal alloy sometimes called Pinchbeck, English, late 19th century. *Maureen McEvoy.*

Two pair of earrings of gild metal alloy sometimes called Pinchbeck, English, circa 1860. *Patricia Funt.*

Earrings of silver with foiled backed paste, French, circa 1800 in open work design. *Kiki McDonough.*

Earrings of gold colored metal alloy, late 19th century. *M. Klein.*

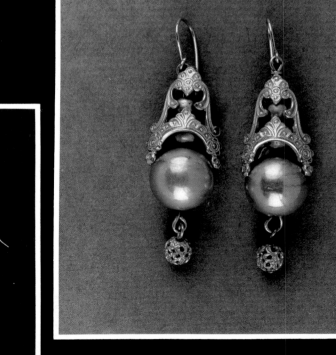

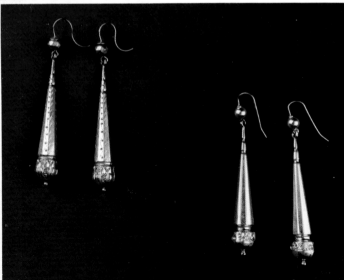

Two necklaces and pin of English origin with colored glass and gold foil backings. *Diana Foley.*

Necklace of gold colored metal alloy sometimes called Pinchbeck with yellow glass pastes prong set with open backs. English, circa 1890. *Kiki McDonough.*

Pendant necklace of rhinestones and silver in a design representative of the Edwardian period in England, circa 1910. *Maureen McEvoy.*

break for the waist, and soft, easy falls of thin pastel colored fabrics. Hem lines again rose to tease at the bottom of the knee. In the 1920's Egyptian designs were revived by Howard Carter's discoveries, including King Tutankhamon's tomb, in Egypt's Valley of the Kings in 1922.

Travel to exotic places became popular for the very rich fashion-setters in the 1920's. After French jeweler Louis Cartier returned from a safari to Africa, he designed animal pins, including his very famous panther jewelry. These designs have been copied and re-interpreted world-wide ever since, giving rise to figural "scatter" pins of all descriptions. Many examples follow in the section on pins.

Short sleeves became usual in clothing, freeing the arm for bracelets which became tremendously popular in the 1920's. Popular, too, for the first time was a suntan, which had formerly been a sign of working in the fields; but now it signified freedom from clothes and a more relaxed life style.

In the 1920's, too, hair styles became short and angular. As a result, earrings of long, drop design were the perfect dramatic touch. Cloche hats were popular for day and evening wear alike. Longer waists made long strands of beads, pearls or chain the perfect complement to the new styles.

Advances being made in the world of plastics had a enormous effect on jewelry. Advertisements from the 1920-23 period shown here depict some of the early costume jewelry designs for Bakelite plastics. Its moldable and coloring properties have made plastic an increasingly more important material for jewelry as the century has progressed.

Bakelite and Lucite marine life pins, circa 1930-1940. *Karen Carmichael and Wendy Tyson.*

Advertisement for Bakelite earrings in a promotional brochure of The Embed Art Company, circa 1923.

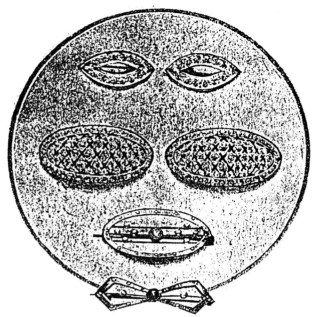

(230) *The topmost buckles are tiny affairs of aluminum set with rhinestones, and each has a pin at its back; ¾ in. long; $1 a pair.* (231) *The more imposing buckles just below are also set with rhinestones; 1¼ in. long; $5.50 a pair.* (232) *Next to the bottom is an oval brooch of gold, set with tiny pearls and a single diamond; 1 in. long; $13.50.* (233) *At the bottom is a gold brooch in the form of a bow-knot, with tiny circles cut in the gold. It is set with two little pearls and one tourmaline; 1 in. long; $5*

Advertisement for rhinestone jewelry from the December 1, 1916 issue of *Vogue* magazine.

By 1925 Art Deco styles of geometric lines and bold colors were firmly established as the most popular fashion look among the wealthy and fashionable clients. Evening dresses were frequently ornamented with elaborate beadwork—which was actually a form of costume jewelry itself. Diamonds set in platinum and colored stones set in gold became standard for real jewelry, and imitations in glass stones were made in abundance. Besides glass, during this period, alternate forms of imitation stones were investigated. Natural crystals were used when large and particularly brilliant effects were required, and the best of these came from Austria, Bohemia and Czechoslovakia. The workmanship of crystals and fine glass stones in these areas is still highly regarded today. Natural crystals from the bottom of the river Rhine in Germany were early substitutes for diamonds, especially in smaller sizes. The popularity of these coined the term "rhinestone" which today is used to mean any imitation stone, usually of glass, either clear or colored.

From the 1930's widespread taxation and quickly changing business situations brought a dramatic change in the clientele of the leading fashion houses. Fewer Royal and Social occasions called for formal wear. Women were starting to work to help family incomes.

In the 1930's costume jewelry became ever more accepted and common as the prices for real jewelry were well beyond the majority of incomes. Hard times fell for many people, but mass-produced costume jewelry helped brighten a smile in the midst of dreary prospects. Sometimes a new dress was out of the question, but a pretty pin would pick up the spirits. This was the time of enormous advancement and expansion for the costume

Link bracelet of carved blue crystal and rhinestones, circa 1950. *Angela Kramer, Inc.*

Link bracelet of silver base metal and blue cabochon glass, circa 1940's. *Angela Kramer, Inc.*

# ASPREY & CO., LTD.

## IMITATION JEWELLERY

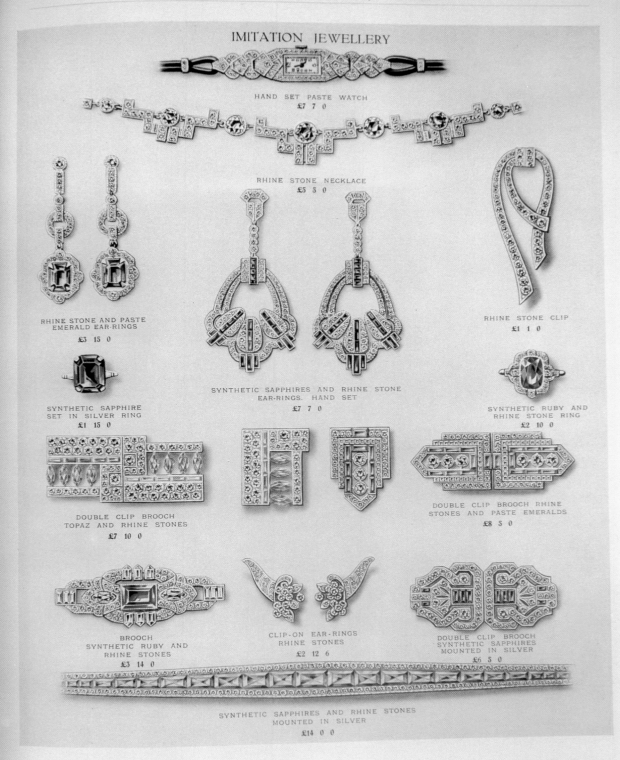

HAND SET PASTE WATCH
£7 7 0

RHINE STONE NECKLACE
£5 5 0

RHINE STONE AND PASTE
EMERALD EAR-RINGS
£3 15 0

SYNTHETIC SAPPHIRES AND RHINE STONE
EAR-RINGS. HAND SET
£7 7 0

RHINE STONE CLIP
£1 1 0

SYNTHETIC SAPPHIRE
SET IN SILVER RING
£1 15 0

SYNTHETIC RUBY AND
RHINE STONE RING
£2 10 0

DOUBLE CLIP BROOCH
TOPAZ AND RHINE STONES
£7 10 0

DOUBLE CLIP BROOCH RHINE
STONES AND PASTE EMERALDS
£8 5 0

BROOCH
SYNTHETIC RUBY AND
RHINE STONES
£3 14 0

CLIP-ON EAR-RINGS
RHINE STONES
£2 12 6

DOUBLE CLIP BROOCH
SYNTHETIC SAPPHIRES
MOUNTED IN SILVER
£6 5 0

SYNTHETIC SAPPHIRES AND RHINE STONES
MOUNTED IN SILVER
£14 0 0

Gold and silver mesh jewelry by Trifari, circa 1970.

Opposite:
Page from an Asprey & Co. Ltd. catalog, London, circa 1930, showing "imitation jewelry" with "synthetic" colored stones and "rhinestones".

jewelry industry. Major designers such as Chanel and Schiaparelli competed fiercely to produce jewelry designs for authentic as well as inexpensive styles, as they recognized the potential of the mass population versus the dwindling number of wealthy clients. Schiaparelli used buttons of all types as ornaments—not merely as fastenings. Chanel used pins as part of her design concepts—not merely as accent pieces. She also coined the word "costume" to describe her designs which were accompanied by all their accessories as a complete fashion look. The hat, jewelry, handbag and clothing all together made up her "costumes."

Fashions in the 1930's brought bias cut, clinging dresses with no sleeves and low backs. Jewelry was designed to enhance the face, so necklaces became extremely popular, turning up in a wide variety of styles and materials. Bugs, birds and animals appeared in figural pins which became important fashion accessories. Plastics continued to be utilized for their bright colors and low cost molded settings which were produced in mass numbers. Earrings were very popular, especially the long dangling styles which echoed the long, slinky, swinging styles of the clothes. The World's Fair in 1939 in New York predicted futuristic designs in architecture using sky scrapers as a new theme.

By the end of the 1930's the tubular, soft clothing styles were replaced by wide shouldered, short skirted and tight waisted designs. Angles were again the desired appearance. At the same time, luxury items became vulgar as the world prepared for war. Rations went into effect in Europe from 1941, and many fabrics and metals such as platinum were requisitioned for military purposes.

In real jewelry, gold and silver were used for settings which were designed with a lot of metal showing. Less important stones were used because the supply of gems from the Orient was cut off. In recent years the term "Retro" has been applied to jewelry of the 1940's, being coined apparently by a major auction house when describing this jewelry in their catalogs. It is thought the term Retro was meant to sound like "Deco" (as in Art Deco style) and connote the evolution of the style from that of the late 1920's.

The costume jewelry industry at this time used rhodium in the alloy for settings. A cousin element to platinum but far less valuable and more available, rhodium is brittle and has little luster, but was a suitable material under the circumstances.

After the Second World War, in 1946, designers once again had the use of ample quantities and varieties of fabrics with which to work, and they made clothing with softer lines, with longer and fuller skirts. Costume jewelry designs continued to be conservative.

In the spring of 1947 the French house of Dior introduced their "New Look" with full and graceful longer skirts, curved shoulders and tiny waists. Shape was again important, and this look became instantly popular among all designers. In 1954 Chanel introduced long gold chains with colored stones scattered through—which was immediately popular in the costume jewelry field.

The 1950's went through many revival styles of the previous half century. For example, from Art Deco originals, fringe and pendant necklaces became popular once more, and elaborate jeweled collars took a prominant place reminiscent of the late 1920's styles. Necklaces became the most important form of jewelry in the 1950's, for tiaras were passé by this time.

The good times of the 1950's set the tone for well dressed women to be immaculately groomed, carefully dressed, and fitted with the correct accessories: shoes, belt, hat and jewelry coordinated. The costume jewelry field once again hit new levels of both volume and quality. Sets of matching jewelry were common perhaps expected. Many examples appear in the following sections. Rings, earrings, bracelets and necklaces must match. Handbags, umbrellas, gloves and scarves all were coordinated. Perhaps the word Costume was used in its most broad definition describing the look of the 1950's.

In 1964 the French house of Courreges made fashion history by its revolutionary Spring Collection. Here were youth-oriented short skirts and loose fitting styles of stiff fabrics with geometric shapes. Bright, cheerful, youthful colors became the norm. High boots and mini-skirts were fun for the young. The fashion houses recognized the young as new, less affluent customers and expanded their boutique and ready-to-wear markets to attract them. No sooner were designers' new styles shown to the public, than copies were available in the ready-to-wear markets. In the late 1960's a fashion developed for "hot pants"—short and tight fitting, brightly colored pants which exposed as much leg as possible.

Costume jewelry in the 1960's also became liberated from tradition, as bold designs in a myriad of materials were available from a new wave of Craft artists who thought independently. Influenced by space exploration and the dream of world peace, fashion designs reflected many moods. Originally designed enameled metal pins and bracelets in bright colors became fashionable. Necklaces and pins in many figural forms were also popular. Strobe lighting was popularized by entertainment preferences by the young for rock band music, which utilized strong and changing lights during their performances. For these entertainers, flashing jewelry matched their moods.

As though the pendulum of change were predictably returning through its swing, the popular styles of the 1970's returned to soft fabrics neatly layered, long skirt with small prints, and gentle shapes. The demure look of peasant dresses was a welcome relief to some who found the extreme styles of the 1960's unflattering. In the 1970's however, there remained the opportunity for a wide choice in fashion styles. Individualism in clothing style was more important than accepting any one look. Therefore, many varieties of clothing and jewelry remained popular. Reinterpretations of Renaissance and Art Deco styling co-existed with futuristic designs in plastics, metals, and other new materials. Hard edge designs were popular in one group, while the flower children parading in sandaled feet wore garlands in another group.

In the 1980's, decorated tee shirts and sweat shirts have captured wide appeal as a very casual, leisure time oriented life style predominates. Wide-cut dresses and shirts are coupled with full pants in crushable fabrics.

While the majority of customers now choose their jewelry from the costume group, they also support an expanding market of antique and modern gem-set jewelry. The modern business men and women recognize badges of success such as real gems and gold jewelry during work hours, while leisure time is spent in casual clothes with imaginative inexpensive jewelry.

Much new costume jewelry today is found in over sized designs, of solid metal and with brightly colored patterns which call attention to the individual. "Notice Me" the jewelry relates. But is that different from jewelry's role at any other age?

Gold colored metal jewelry by Trifari, circa 1960.

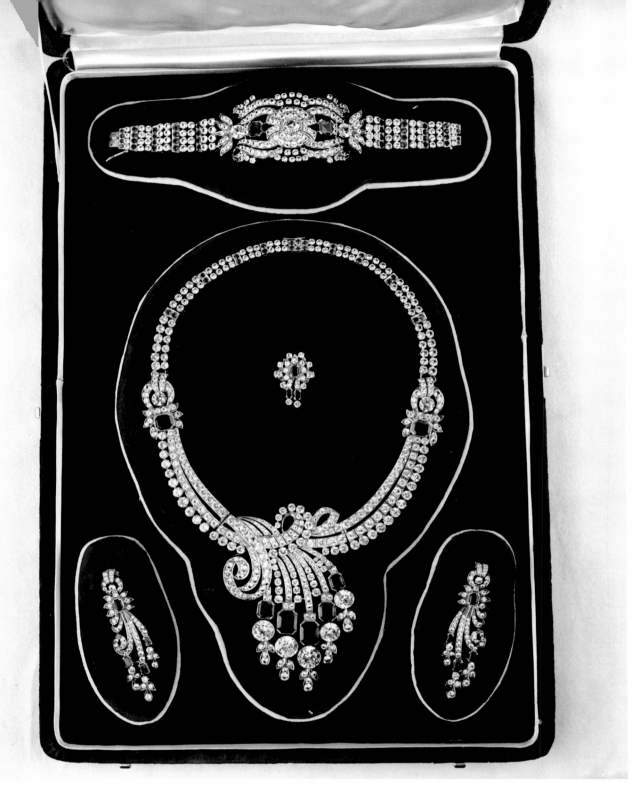

Parure including bracelet, necklace, ring and earrings in original box, unsigned, mid-twentieth century. *Norman Crider.*

Opposite:
Parure including pin, earrings, necklace and bracelet, unsigned, mid-twentieth century by Kramer for Christian Dior, apparently shown at one of his first fashion shows in America in the 1940's. *Jackie Fleischmann.*

# Matching Sets

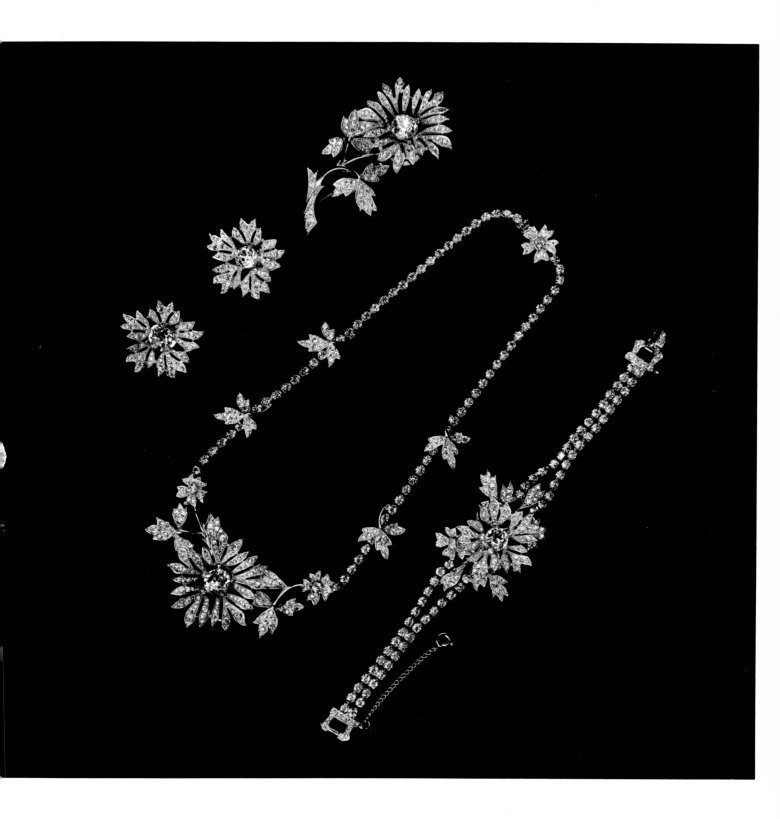

Parure including bracelet, necklace and earrings by Miriam Haskell, circa 1950. Miriam Haskell (1899-1981) was an elegant artist who began selling jewelry when she ran a gift shop in 1924 in the McAlpin Hotel at Herald Square, New York. She moved to West 57th Street where she supervised production of her costume jewelry as designed by Frank Hess, and in 1933 moved again to 392 Fifth Avenue where she remained until the 1960's. Most of her pieces were marked from the 1930's onward with an oval plate stamped "Miriam Haskell." Now under private ownership, the company continues today. *Norman Crider.*

Parure by Harper including earrings, pendant or pin, and bangle bracelet in open wire work design. *Dennis Cogdell.*

Parure by Trifari, 1940's, designed to emulate red garnet jewelry of the late 19th century with Austrian glass set in sterling silver.

Parure including jabot pin, bird pin, earrings, bracelet, and two floral pins by Trifari, 1930's. The silver settings have carved colored stones set in silver to emulate Indian style designs for gem set jewelry made and popularized by Louis Cartier in the late 1920's. The firm of Trifari (officially Trifari, Krussman & Fiskel) was begun in 1925 in Providence, Rhode Island and quickly gained a leadership roll in the costume jewelry field. The company continues today. *Bizarre Bazaar.*

Parure including a link bracelet and a bangle bracelet (see left), four pins and long drop earrings by Trifari, 1950's. This design is a new interpretation of the Indian style jewelry made by Tirfari in the 1930's (see previous page) with gold alloy settings and cabuchon colored stones. *Norman Crider.*

Parure including pin, earrings and bracelet by Schiaparelli, circa 1950, with light green cut crystals in gold colored alloy. The house of Schiaparelli closed in 1954. *Muriel Karasik.*

Parure including bracelet, neck
lace and earrings by Hobé. The
Hobé family has been in the
jewelry manufacturing business
since the late 19th century. In
1889, Jacques Hobé made
affordable jewelry in Paris. His
son William came to New York
in 1903 and established the
modern firm based on the
designs of Sylvia Hobé. Today
the company continues under
direction of William's sons
Donald and Robert. The following cartouches around the name
Hobé identify the period of manu-
facture:

1903-1917

1918-1932

1933-1957

1958-present

*Terry Rogers*

Parure including earrings,
pendant and ring distributed by
Sarah Coventry circa 1960. The
stones are set in silver. The
Sarah Coventry firm was established by C. H. Stuart & Co. as
a disbributor of costume jewelry
in 1950. It was associated with
the Emmous Jewelers, Inc. of
Newark, New Jersey. *Franny's.*

Parure including hinged bangle
bracelet, pin and earrings of
enameled silver by Matisse,
1960's. *Jackie Fleischmann.*

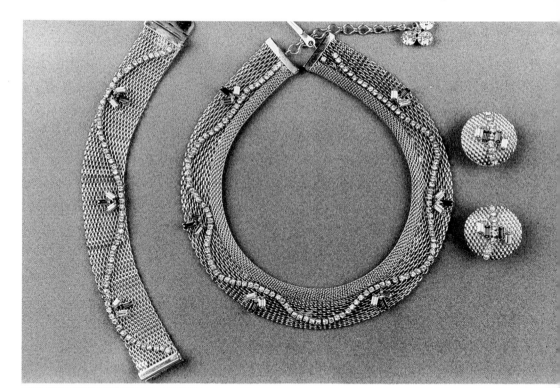

Opposite: Parure including necklace, earrings and bracelet of prong-set, colored and foil backed glass stones, unsigned, circa 1960. *Norman Crider.*

Parure including necklace, earrings and bracelet, by Kramer, circa 1960. *Jackie Fleischmann.*

Parure including necklace, earrings and bracelet with pearl, clear, and iridescent red glass stones in white pit metal, unsigned, circa 1965. *Jackie Fleischmann.*

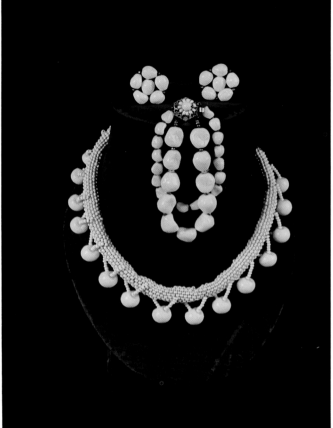

Necklace and earrings by Kenneth J. Lane, circa 1970, of clear glass set in black enamel.

Parure including earrings, bracelet and necklace by Miriam Haskell, circa 1950. *Michael & Matthew.*

Opposite:
Parure including necklace, bracelet and earrings by Schreiner, New York, circa 1960. *Norman Crider.*

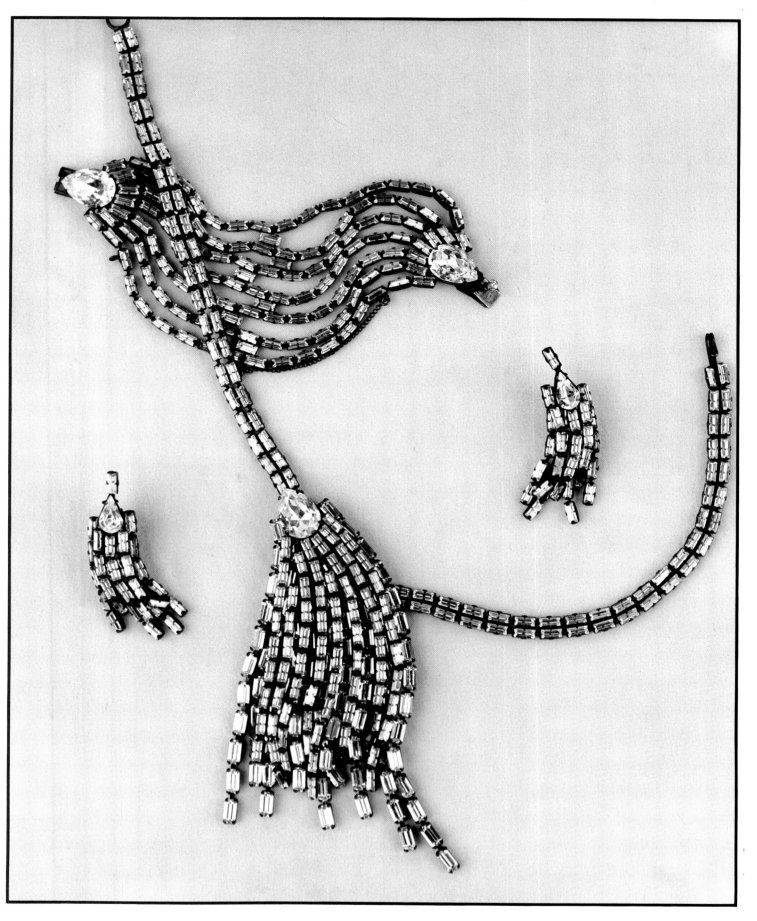

Choker of gold colored metal alloy mesh with pink foiled crystals, English, late eighteenth century. Necklace of light blue foiled stones linked with metal rings supporting a detachable matching pendant, English, late eighteenth century. *Patricia Funt.*

Choker with a long back pendant of green glass beads and rhinestone rondels, French, c. 1925. *Bizarre Bazaar.*

# Necklaces

## Chokers

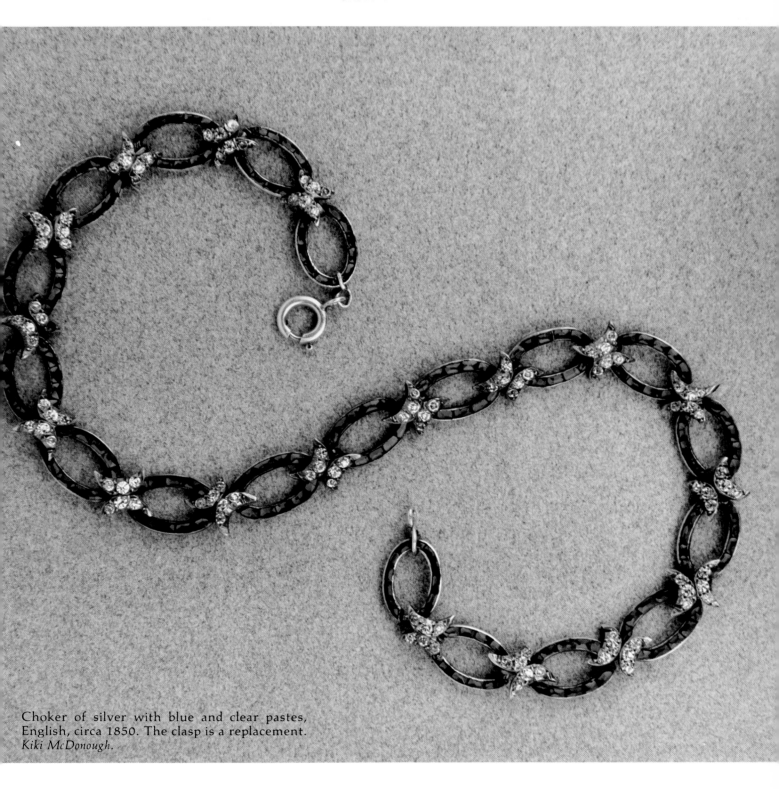

Choker of silver with blue and clear pastes, English, circa 1850. The clasp is a replacement. *Kiki McDonough.*

Choker of brown woven rope with colored wooden beads as leaves, Czechoslovakian, circa 1960. *Muriel Karasik.*

Choker and earrings of gold colored metal alloy chains, leaves and tassel fringe by De Mario of New York, circa 1960. *Terry Rogers.*

Choker is classical Roman style of gold colored metal alloy leaves by Miriam Haskell, circa 1930, *Muriel Karasik.*

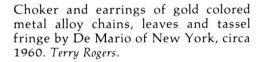

Choker of blue and clear carved glass beads, c.
1930. Pair of dress clips with blue glass cabuchons
and rhinestones. Pin of bird design with enamels
and rhinestones. *Ann's Art.*

Opposite page:
Choker of red cord with colored wooden beads as flowers and pots, Czechoslovakian, circa 1960. *Muriel Karasik.*

Choker of gold colored metal alloy and false grey pearls by Miriam Haskell, circa 1950. *Muriel Karasik.*

Choker of gold filled metal with clear crystals and tiny false pearls, unsigned. *Muriel Karasik.*

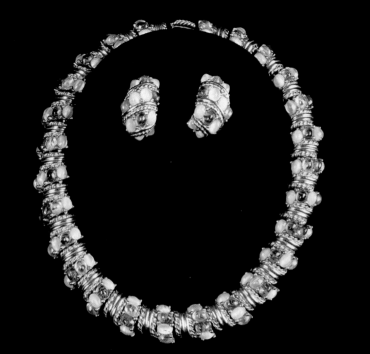

Choker of rhinestones in linked silver metal mesh by Ciner, New York, circa 1950. The Ciner family worked in real jewelry from 1892 to 1931 when they began producing costume designs. The stones were of finest quality imported from Germany and Eastern Europe. The family-run business continues. *Norman Crider.*

Choker and earrings with colored cabochon glass stones by Boucher, c. 1960. *Matthew and Michael.*

Opposite:
Choker and earrings of silver colored snake chain with rhinestone set links by Kenneth J. Lane, circa 1970. Kenneth J. Lane designed shoe decorations in New York before starting his own costume jewelry firm in 1963. He has produced a large quantity of fine quality designs.

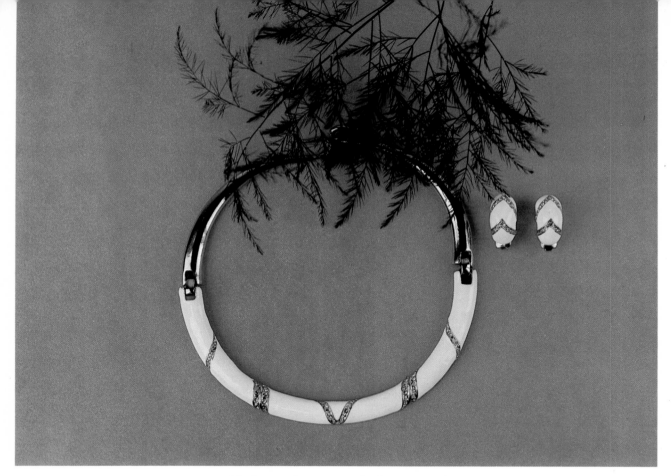

Choker and earrings of white enamel on gold colored metal alloy with rhinestones by Kenneth J. Lane, circa, 1975.

Unsigned choker and earrings by Miriam Haskell of clear plastic beads and filigree gold colored metal chain, circa 1960. *M. Klein.*

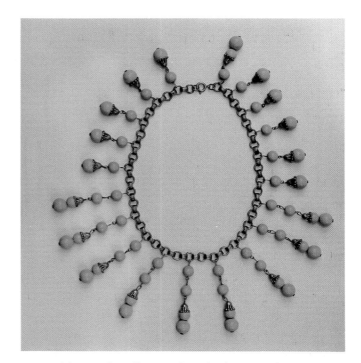

Necklace of colored glass beads on silver chain backing, unsigned, 1950's. *Matthew and Michael.*

Necklace of gold colored cast metal and colored glass beads in classical style, circa 1940. *Dennis Cogdell.*

Necklace of yellow colored chain and green Bakelite plastic beads, circa 1930. *Jackie Fleischmann.*

Choker and earrings of silver with blue enamels by Boucher, circa 1960. *Terry Rogers.*

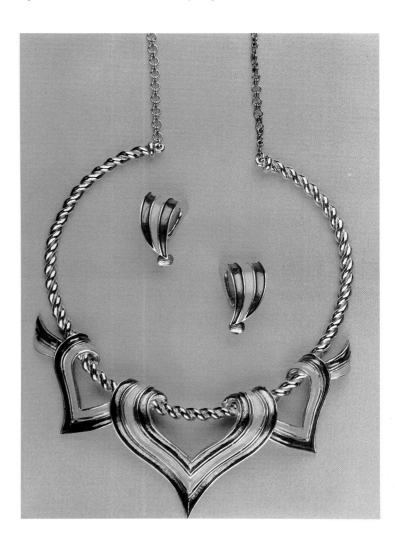

Necklace of rhinestones by Pinnetta, circa 1960. *Michael and Matthew.*

Necklace and bracelet of rhinestones, maker unknown, circa 1985. *Michael and Matthew.*

Necklace of sterling with rhinestones by Phyllis made to have the ends dangle down the back, circa 1960. *Ronnie Seigle.*

Opposite page:
Necklace and earrings of rhinestones, maker unknown, circa 1985. *Matthew and Michael.*

Choker and earrings of rhinestones, maker unknown, circa 1970. *Lorraine Matt.*

Choker and earrings of rhodium plated metal with Eastern European crystals marked "Eisenberg Ice", circa 1955. *Matthew and Michael.*

Necklace and earrings of rhinestones, circa 1970. *Matthew and Michael.*

Necklace of tinted and foil backed rhinestones, maker unknown, circa 1955. *Bob Coyle and Marianne Ward.*

Choker of clear and green iridescent glass beads, by Coppola Toppo, Italian, circa 1970. *Muriel Karasik.*

Choker of gold colored wire and colored rhinestones, unknown maker, circa 1960. *Jackie Fleischmann.*

Necklace and earrings with iridescent pink beads in fringe design by Hobé, circa 1950. *Muriel Karasik.*

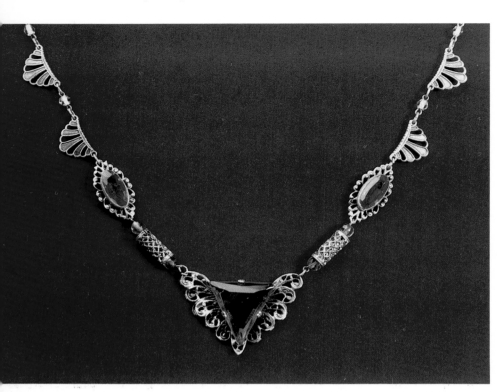

Necklace of plated silver in Hungarian style, circa 1935, maker unknown. *Dennis Cogdell.*

Necklace and earrings of iridescent and blue faceted and cabuchon crystals by Schiaparelli, circa 1940. *Muriel Karasik.*

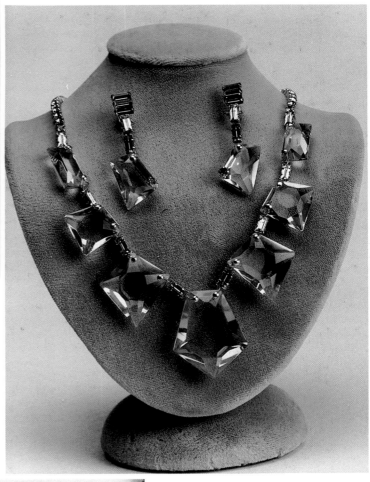

Necklace of rhinestones and blue crystals by an unknown maker, circa 1960. *Michael and Matthew.*

Necklace and earrings of exceptionally large ice blue crystals, maker unknown, circa 1960. *Jackie Fleischmann.*

Necklace and earrings of foil backed glass stones, unknown maker, circa 1940. *Franny's.*

Necklace and earrings of gold filled white metal, blue crystal and rhinestones by Jomaz, circa 1950.
*Norman Crider.*

Necklace of gold filled white metal with red crystal and rhinestones by Jomaz, circa 1945. *Norman Crider.*

Three *Headlight* necklaces of foil backed colored crystals in blue and black mountings by Kenneth J. Lane, circa 1985.

Collar and earrings of colored cabochon glass stones in gold colored metal from Trifari in 1956.

*Let Them Eat Cake* necklace of grey crystal and rhinestones by Kenneth J. Lane, circa 1985.

### Collars

Collar of brown and clear rhinestones with grey and white false pearl drops, maker unknown, circa 1955. *Norman Crider.*

Collar of cut crystal and rhinestones by Kenneth J. Lane, circa 1980.

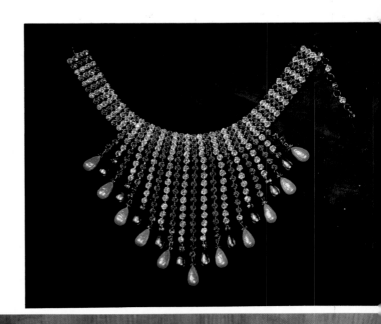

Collar of draped rhinestone strands by an unknown maker, circa 1965. *Matthew and Michael.*

Collar and earrings of clear rhinestones with false pearl drops, maker unknown, circa 1955. *Matthew and Michael.*

Collar and earrings of colored glass and rhinestones set in yellow colored material, maker unknown. *Jackie Fleischmann.*

Collar of gold colored metal and yellow glass beads forming a swarm of bees by Miriam Haskell, 1940's.
*Norman Crider.*

Collar of shaded glass stones in metal backing, unknown maker, circa 1950's. *Ronnie Seigle.*

Collar of red glass beads by Coppola Toppo, Italian, circa 1970. *Muriel Karasik.*

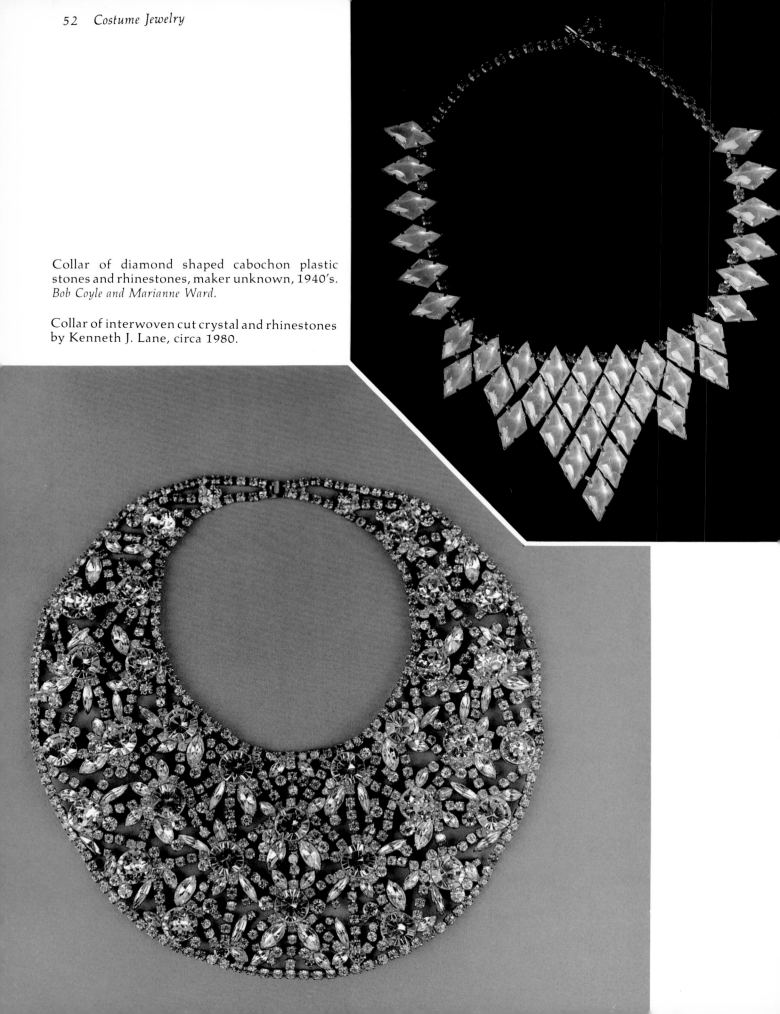

Collar of diamond shaped cabochon plastic stones and rhinestones, maker unknown, 1940's. *Bob Coyle and Marianne Ward.*

Collar of interwoven cut crystal and rhinestones by Kenneth J. Lane, circa 1980.

Collar of linked blue crystal stones in enclosed backs, unsigned, circa 1950's. *Ronnie Seigle.*

Collar of gold colored metal wire and grey false pearls by an unknown maker, circa 1965. *Muriel Karasik*

**Beads**

Necklaces clockwise from top: Multi-strands of white glass beads marked Japan. / Black Venetian glass patterned beads with small spacers. / Clear and black glass beads. / Wired black and white glass beads. / Silver and black glass graduated beads. *M. Klein.*

Necklace of colored glass beads on twisted strand, unsigned, circa 1970. *M. Klein.*

Necklace of colored wooden beads from Czechoslovakia, circa 1960. *Muriel Karasik.*

Necklace and bracelet of coral colored glass beads and rhinestone clusters by Miriam Haskell, 1950's. *Ronnie Seigle.*

Choker of Venetian enameled glass beads on knotted cord, circa 1950. / Choker of faceted crystal beads on knotted cord, circa 1970. *M. Klein.*

Necklace of shaped and polished crystal with rhinestone spacers, unsigned, circa 1970. *Jackie Fleischmann.*

Necklace and earrings with red molded plastic beads and rhinestones by Miriam Haskell, circa 1960. *Norman Crider.*

Opposite page:
Necklace of assorted glass beads, maker unknown, circa 1960. *Marian R. Carroll.*

Earrings, necklace and bracelet of iridescent crystal and rhinestone beads by an unknown maker, circa 1960. *Matthew and Michael.*

Choker necklace of crystal, iridescent and false Baroque pearl beads in a staggared arrangement, maker unknown, circa 1960. *Marian R. Carroll.*

Necklace of glass and metal beads by an unknown maker, circa 1950. *Jackie Fleischmann.*

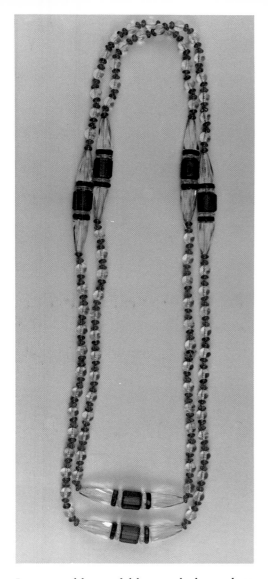

Long necklace of blue and clear glass beads, 1920's. *Jackie Fleischmann.*

Opposite:
Bead necklaces by Kenneth J. Lane, circa 1975. White molded glass beads with initials. / White crackled ceramic beads. / Clear crystals in gold chain links.

Necklace of painted and carved wood to imitate ivory, 1930's. *Dennis Cogdell.*

Long necklace of speckled ceramic beads, 1930's. *Matilda D. Knowles II.*

Long necklace and nearly matching clip style earrings with cut glass and plastic beads and molded yellow colored metal, 1950's. *M. Klein.*

Choker of colored and layered wooden beads made in Czechoslovakia, circa 1960. *Muriel Karasik.*

Long necklace of gold colored metal chain and enameled links, with matching earrings, by Monet, circa 1960. *Jackie Fleischmann.*

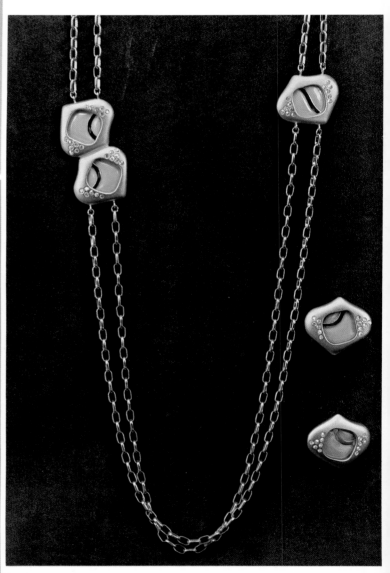

Two necklaces of false Baroque pearls by Miriam Haskell, circa 1950. Single strand opera length and double strand short necklace, each with gold colored small spacers. *Matthew and Michael.*

Choker of small Baroque pearls with gold colored small spacers and bow-tie pendant accented with rhinestones by Miriam Haskell, circa 1940. *Muriel Karasik.*

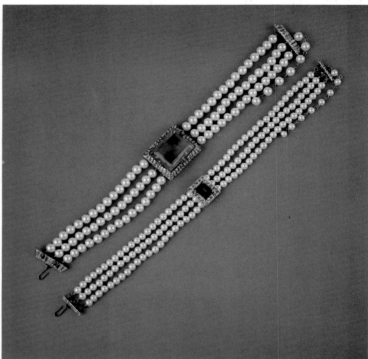

Opera length necklace of knotted false pearls with paisley designed clasp set with colored and rhinestones by Kenneth J. Lane, circa 1980.

Two chokers of false pearls and colored glass stones with rhinestoes by Kenneth J. Lane, circa 1975.

Necklace and earrings with round and Baroque false pearls and rhinestones, maker unknown, circa 1960. *Matthew and Michael.*

Group of pearl necklaces including linked rope in three lengths, twisted strands with decorative clasps and matching earrings, pin and bracelet, and pendants with matching earrings, all by Trifari, circa 1970.

Choker necklace of false pearls and colored glass by Schiaparelli, circa 1945. *M. Klein.*

## Pendant Necklaces

Pendant necklace and bracelet of gold colored metal alloy mesh chain, false pearls and cameo. The bracelet is marked "Patented Sept. 16, 1873." English. *M. Klein.*

Pendant necklace of brass and glass to imitate garnets, made in Eastern Europe, circa 1930. *Dennis Cogdell.*

Pendant necklace of black glass to imitate jet. English or French, circa 1875. Chain added later. *Jackie Fleischmann.*

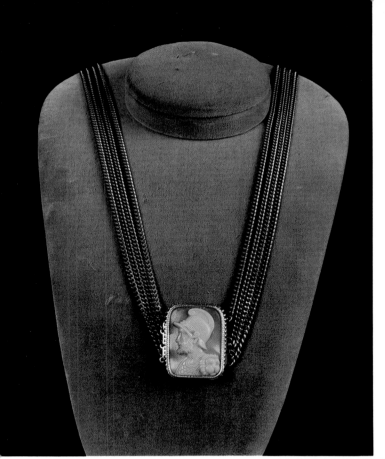

Pendant necklace of gold colored metal chain and cast plastic cameo by Hattie Carnegie, circa 1950. *Matthew and Michael.*

Pendant necklace of gold colored metal and rhinestone set chain with carved glass scarab by Kenneth J. Lane, circa 1975. *Marian R. Carroll.*

Group of pendant and choker necklaces in gold colored metal alloy finish with matching pins and earrings, all made by Trifari circa 1960.

Necklace of rhinestone set chain with three clear glass stones, unsigned, circa 1950. *M. Klein.*

Choker of gold colored metal chain with pendant blue glass in cross mounting, by Nettie Rosenstein, 1950's. *Terry Rogers*

Pendant necklace of gold colored chain and square pendant with coat of arms reading *L. Union fait la force* by Miriam Haskell, 1950's. / Pendant necklace of gold colored chain and round coin representing L. W. M. Von Baden, 1655-1707, as a false 5 Deutschmark coin from the German Democratic Republic, circa 1955. / Sterling silver pendant pin by Nettie Rosenstein of false coins, circa 1955. *Terry Rogers.*

Earrings and two pendant necklaces by Kenneth J. Lane nearly replicating in costume jewelry designs of jeweler Giovanni Bulgari of Italy, 1986.

Opposite:
Pendant necklace and earrings in silver gilt and mother-of-pearl, circa 1930, *Maureen McEvoy.*

Pendant necklace of glass beads and carved medallion colored pink to resemble coral, 1920's. *Dennis Cogdell.*

Pendant necklace and earrings of colored stones and yellow colored metal, Austrian circa 1960. *Bob Coyle and Marianne Ward.*

Pendant necklace of Renaissance revival style in molded metal, enamel and glass beads, from Czechoslovakia, circa 1935. *Muriel Karasik.*

Pin mounted as a pendant necklace and matching earrings with Austrian colored glas, 1960's. *Jackie Fleischmann.*

Pendant necklace of glass beads with carved pendant, unsigned, 1920's. *Dennis Cogdell.*

Pendant necklace of gold filled metal by Kenneth J. Lane, circa 1980.

Pendant necklace of imitation jade and rhinestones, French, 1920's. *Angela Kramer Inc.*

Pendant necklace with a seashell mounted with colored glass stones on a rhinestone chain, with black prongs, by Kenneth J. Lane, circa 1975.

Pendant necklace of yellow colored metal and blue glass in Art Nouveau style, unsigned, circa 1910. *Ann's Arts.*

Pendant necklace of gold colored metal chain and false Baroque pearls with aqua beads and rhinestones, by Miriam Haskell, circa 1950. *Norman Crider.*

Pendant necklace of gold colored metal chain, false Baroque pearls and mother-of-pearl, by Miriam Haskell, circa 1950, *Muriel Karasik*.

Pendant necklace of rhinestones with black prongs by Schiaparelli, circa 1950. *Norman Crider.*

Pendant necklace of rhinestones, maker unknown, circa 1960. *Matthew and Michael.*

Opposite:
Pendant necklace and earrings of false Baroque pearls, gold colored metal and rhinestones by Miriam Haskell, circa 1950. *Jackie Fleischmann.*

Pendant necklace of green and clear rhinestones by Napier, circa 1955. *Muriel Karasik.*

Opposite:
Pendant necklace of colored rhinestones and yellow colored metal by Hobé, circa 1955. *Muriel Karasik.*

Pendant necklace of colored and iridescent glass stones in yellow metal marked Made in Austria, circa 1960. *Muriel Karasik.*

Pendant necklace of glass beads and gold colored metal, unsigned, 1930's. *Bob Coyle and Marianne Ward.*

Opposite:
Pendant necklace of gold colored metal chain and colored glass, by Trifari, 1930's. *Jackie Fleischmann.*

Pendant necklace and earrings of gold colored chain with clear crystals, circa 1925. *Franny's.*

Pendant necklace of colored rhinestones set in yellow metal links and three briolette crystals, circa 1925. *Jackie Fleischmann.*

Pendant necklace of colored rhinestones set in yellow colored metal with filled gold metal drops, circa 1925. *Marian R. Carroll.*

Pendant choker of cast yellow metal and false Baroque pearls, unsigned, 1950's. *Bob Coyle and Marianne Ward.*

Pendant choker of colored glass beads by Coppola Toppo of Italy, circa 1960. *Muriel Karasik.*

Pendant necklace of Egyptian revival style with false turquoise and cast yellow metal, 1930's. *Bob Coyle and Marianne Ward.*

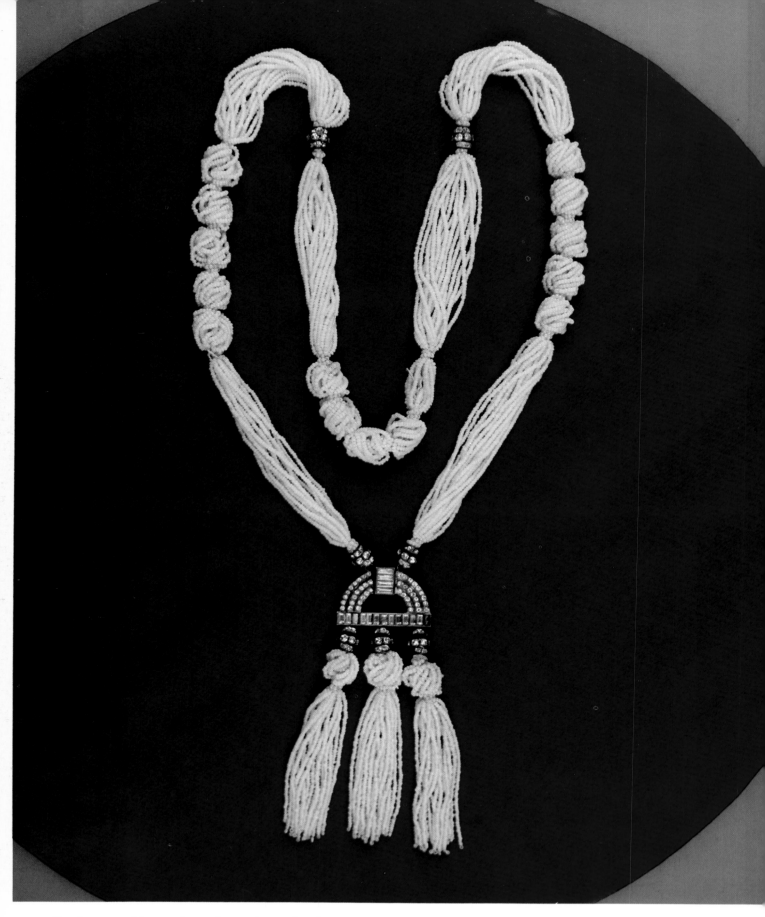

Pendant necklace of seed pearls with rhinestones, French, unsigned, circa 1925. *Angela Kramer, Inc.*

# Bracelets

*Link Bracelets*

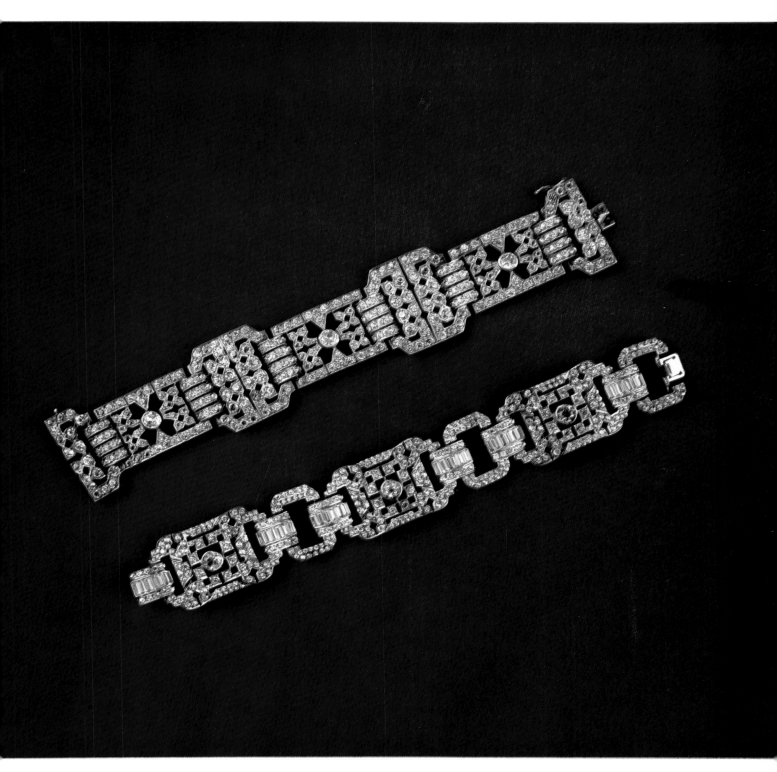

Two link bracelets of silver set with rhinestones, French, 1930's. *Bizarre Bazaar.*

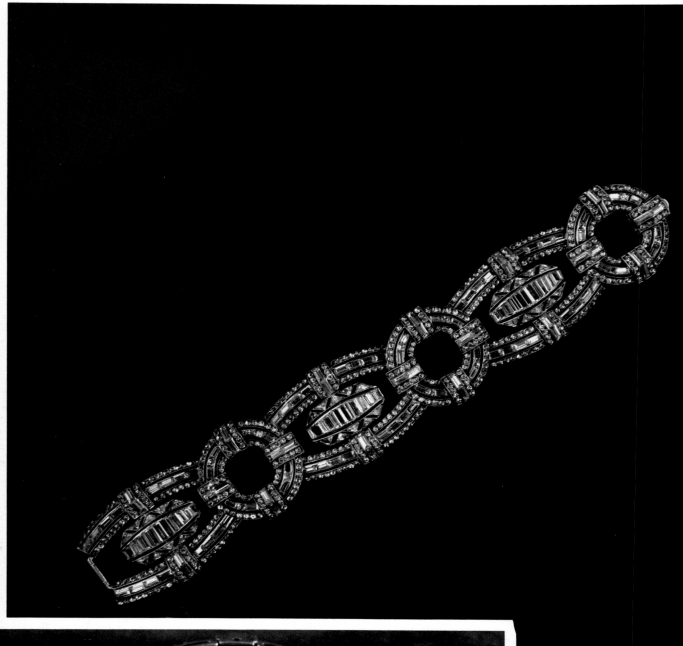

Two views of a German 895 silver link bracelet finely made perhaps as a demonstration of technical skill with open-backed rhinestones, 1930's. *Angela Kramer, Inc.*

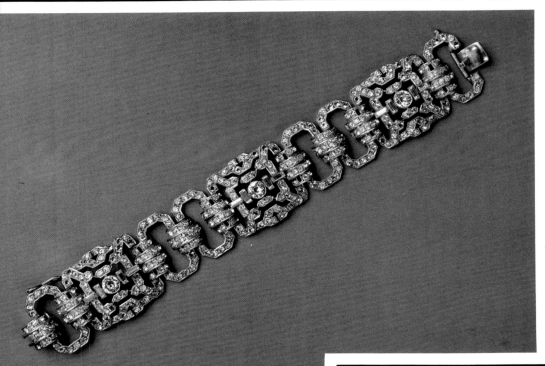

Link bracelet with crystal stones marked Eisenberg Ice, 1950's. *Matthew and Michael.*

Bracelet of blue and clear rhinestones in an expansion band, unmarked, 1960's. *Matthew and Michael.*

Link bracelet of sterling silver with hand set rhinestones and French hallmarks, 1920's. *Michael Greenberg.*

Link bracelet of clear rhinestones set in silver by Robért, 1960's. *Matthew and Michael.*

Brooch of silver set with rhinestones that detaches to form two clips, circa 1940. / Link bracelet of silver with rhinestones and false coral in Art Deco design. / Pin of silver with rhinestones and blue plastic ball in Art Deco design, circa 1935. *Patricia Funt.*

Three link bracelets with rhinestones by Kenneth J. Lane, circa 1980. Top, designed to copy the type made popular in diamonds by Louis Cartier in the 1920's. / Seven diamond shaped links in Art Deco style. / Articulated link design.

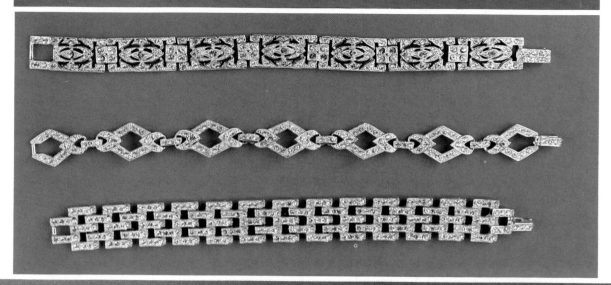

Link bracelet of rhinestones, green glass and enamel in Art Deco design, circa 1925. *Linda Morgan.*

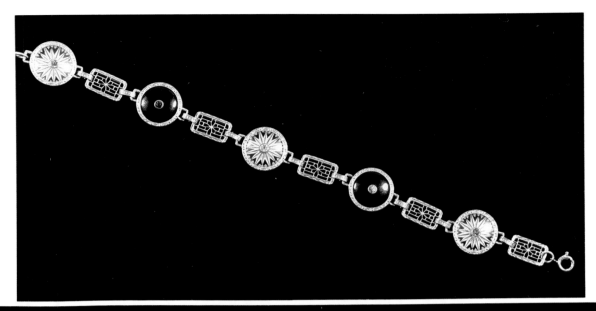

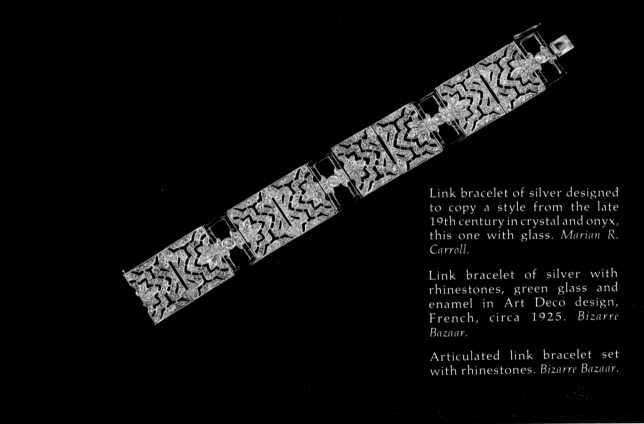

Link bracelet of silver designed to copy a style from the late 19th century in crystal and onyx, this one with glass. *Marian R. Carroll.*

Link bracelet of silver with rhinestones, green glass and enamel in Art Deco design, French, circa 1925. *Bizarre Bazaar.*

Articulated link bracelet set with rhinestones. *Bizarre Bazaar.*

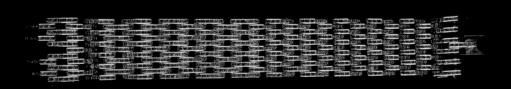

Link bracelet of silver set with paste stones and gold engraved plates, French, circa 1880. *Kiki McDonough.*

Link bracelet of colored glass and rhinestones, unsigned, circa 1940. *Muriel Karasik.*

Link bracelet with colored glass by Schiaparelli, 1930's. *Norman Crider.*

Link bracelet of gold colored metal, grey false pearls and rhinestones, unsigned, circa 1950. *Muriel Karasik.*

Link bracelet set with colored glass, rhinestones and enamel by Trifari, circa 1950. *Jackie Fleischmann.*

Link bracelet and brooch of colored and carved glass and rhinestones designed after a famous style with real gems by Louis Cartier, these unsigned, 1930's. *Muriel Karasik.*

Three link bracelets of gold colored filigree and colored glass by Hobé, circa 1910. *Norman Crider.*

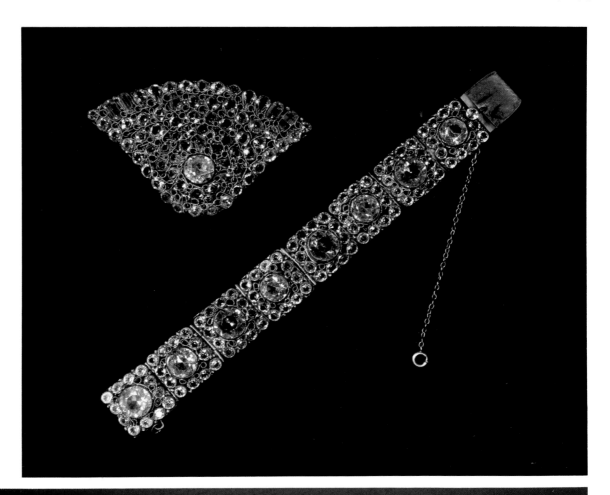

Brooch and link bracelet of gold colored filigree wire and colored glass, made by Hobé circa 1910. *Norman Crider.*

Link bracelet and brooch of colored glass and rhinestones by Trifari, late 1950's. *Norman Crider.*

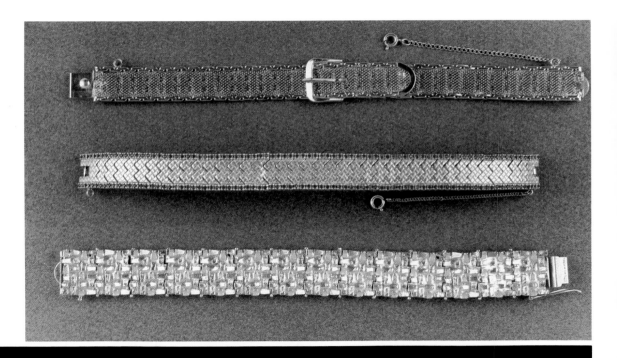

Three link bracelets of gold colored metal, circa 1950. Top, 12k gold filled mesh. / Mesh band with two lines of red glass stones by Ciner. / Nugget finished links by Eton. *M. Klein.*

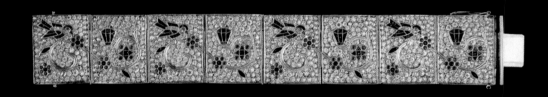

Link bracelet of silver with pavé set colored and clear rhinestoens, circa 1940. *Bizarre Bazaar.*

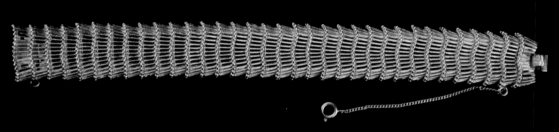

Link bracelet of gilt metal by Sandra Boucher, 1960's. *Angela Kramer, Inc.*

Link bracelet of silver and colored glass marked Eisenberg Ice, circa 1955. *Ronnie Seigle.*

Link bracelet of silver and enamel with colored glass, circa 1930. *Muriel Karasik.*

Link bracelet in Victorian design gold colored metal with false cameo, circa 1950. *M. Klein.*

Link bracelet of cast gold colored metal with enameled ceramic medallions, three open as lockets, marked Art, circa 1960. *Marian R. Carroll.*

Pin and link bracelet of sterling silver with amethyst colored glass by Cini, circa 1950. *Ronnie Seigle.*

Silver pin of wagon design with enameled flowers set with colored rhinestones circa 1950. / Gold colored metal pin designed to imitate fine Victorian stick pins and a thimble, circa 1960. / Link bracelet of gold colored wire mesh in bow shapes, unsigned, circa 1960. *Muriel Karasik.*

Link bracelet with foil backed glass stones and rhinestones by Schiaparelli, circa 1950. *M. Klein.*

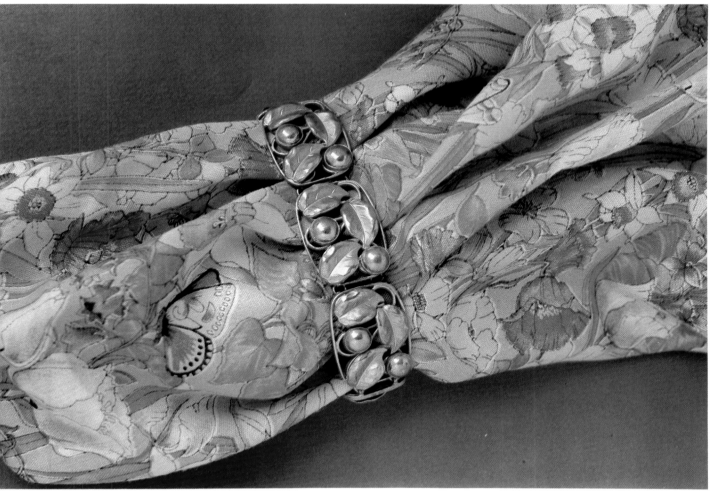

Link bracelet of gilt metal in leaf and berry design, circa 1925. *Linda Morgan.*

Link bracelet of cast gold colored metal with enamel and rhinestones, unsigned, circa 1960. *Muriel Karasik.*

Four link bracelets of pot metal and brass with colored glass mosaics made in Italy, India and China in the tradition of ancient and revival stone mosaic work, circa 1955. *Franny's.*

Link bracelet of gold washed sterling silver with stone carved as scarabs, circa 1950. *Rebecca Frey.*

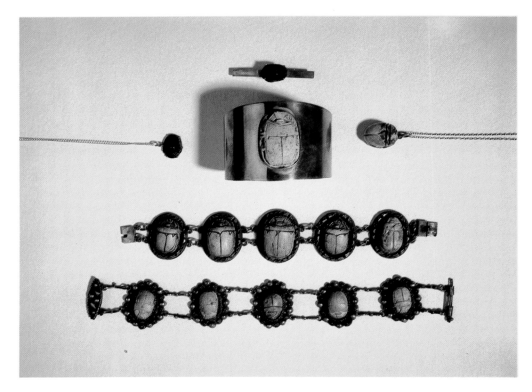

Group of Scarab jewelry including dried scarab beetles in bar pin and pendant, and stone carved scarabs set in bangle bracelet, pendant, and two link bracelets, 1930's. *Ann's Arts.*

Colored glass scarabs set into four silver link bracelets, earrings and pin, circa 1950's. *Franny's.*

## Bangle Braclets

Bangle bracelet and earrings of colored glass beads and iridescent rhinestones by Hobé, circa 1950. *Matthew and Michael.*

Eight strand wired pearl bracelet, unsigned, circa 1950. *Matthew and Michael.*

Bangle bracelet of cast gold colored metal and carved smoky amethyst quartz, circa 1920. *Matthew and Michael.*

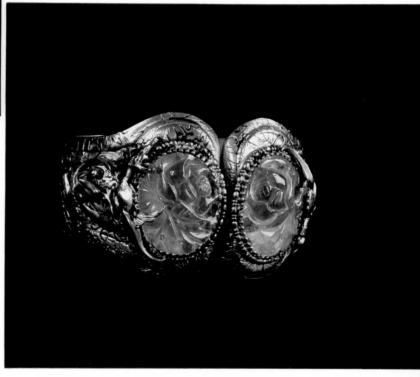

Bracelet of colored wooden beads on elastic band from Czechoslovakia, circa 1960. *Muriel Karasik.*

Bangle bracelet of colored and foil backed glass and solid band by Alice Caviness, circa 1970. *Matthew and Michael.*

Hinged bangle bracelet of cast gold colored metal and colored glass, unsigned, circa 1930's. *Jackie Fleischmann.*

Bangle bracelet in the form of a snake with enameled and pavé set rhinestones by Kenneth J. Lane, circa 1970, *Matthew and Michael.*

Bangle bracelet cast as a horse's head by P. Rader, circa 1970. *Matthew and Michael.*

Group of bangle bracelets, earrings and rings set with plastic stones, enamels and rhinestones by Kenneth J. Lane, circa 1975.

Hinged bangle bracelet cast in yellow metal as a snake with green stone eyes by Kenneth J. Lane, circa 1970. *Ronnie Seigle.*

Hinged bangle bracelet of cast yellow metal and enamels by Jomaz, circa 1970. *Terry Rogers.*

Bangle bracelets from the 1950's and 1960's display African ethnic jewelry influences in massive forms and large stones. *Franny's.*

# *Pins*

### *Figural Designs*

Figural pins evolved gradually from the late 19th century gaining popularity and imaginative design as new materials were explored. The sampling shown here represents the wide variety that abounds. This group of planes in silver and pavé rhinestones and a cast sailing ship were made in the 1950's. They are rarely signed *Franny's.*

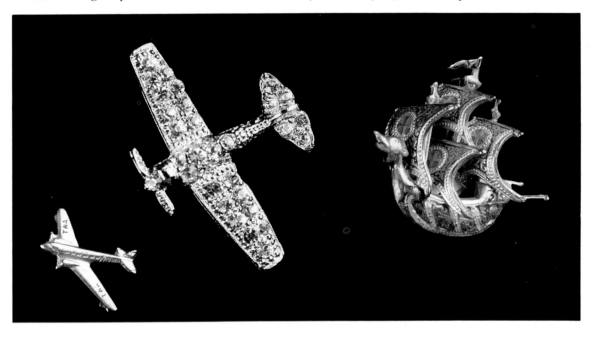

Wooden dog with brass collar and glass eye. *Dennis Cogdell.*

Bob-cat of enameled brass with rhinestones by Panetta. *Terry Rogers.*

Birds comprise a large number of figural pins in a wide variety of styles and materials. Silver and rhinestone eagle, c. 1920. *Maureen McEvoy.*

Unsigned figural pins from the 1950's and 1960's. *M. Klein.*

Gold washed sterling silver, enamel and rhinestone bird by Corocraft, 1950's. *Muriel Karasik.*

Running ostrich of silver, enamel and rhinestones. *Linda Morgan.*

Small figural pins from the 1950's. *Franny's.*

Owls are a popular subject in small pins. *Franny's.*

Imaginary birds from the 1960's. *Terry Rogers.*

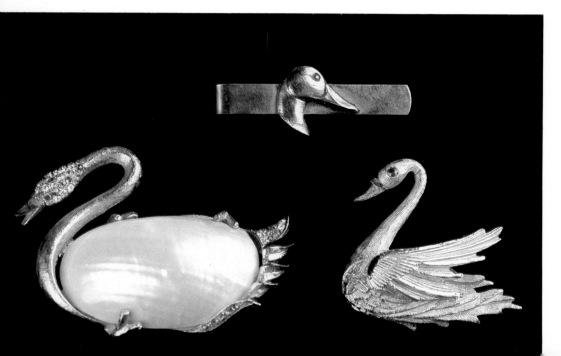

Wildfowl for the man and the ladies. *Franny's.*

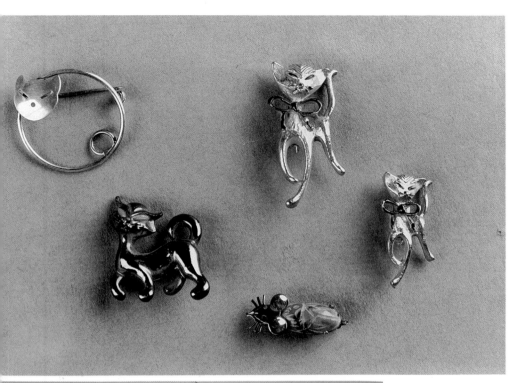

Cats surveying the mouse, 1950's. *Franny's.*

Horses. *Franny's.*

Ann's Arts.

Clips and earrings of an elegant horse head by Corocraft. *Jackie Fleischmann.*

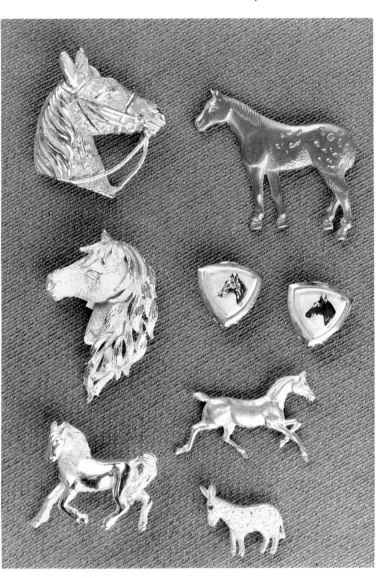

Dogs for the sport of it and for adoring owners.

*Bizarre Bazaar*

*Franny's.*

*Lorraine Matt*

Elephants who never forget. *Muriel Karasik.*

The use of new materials was daring. *Muriel Karasik.*

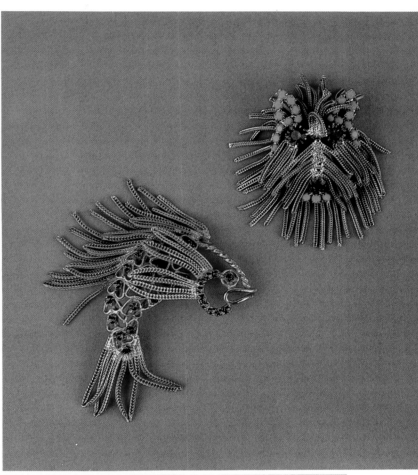

*Maureen McEvoy.*

*Franny's.*

Late Victorian paste-set figural pins were the fore-runners of the popular styles. *Bizarre Bazaar.*

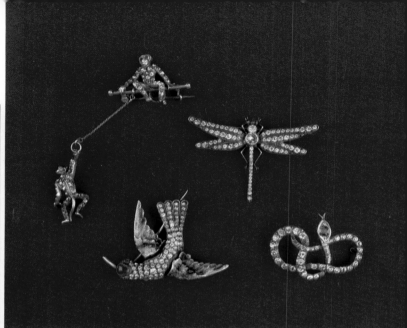

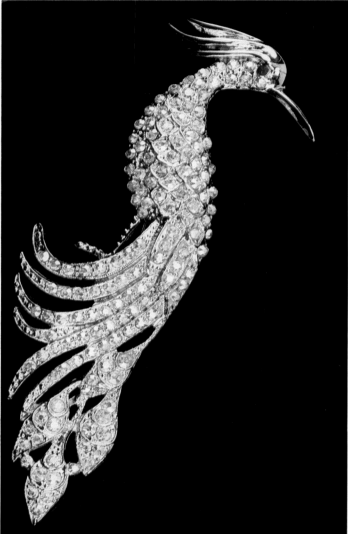

Large iridescent pavé bird, unsigned. *Jackie Fleischmann.*

The pearl-eating crocodile was made by Corocraft, 1950's. *Bizarre Bazaar.*

Dragonfly and purple-breasted bird, unsigned, coral enameled snail by Hattie Carnegie. *Jackie Fleischmann.*

Butterfly in ephemeral shaded tones. *Rebecca Frey.*

Early 20th century French dragonfly of elegant delicacy. Photograph by Steven Mark Needham. *Bizarre Bazaar.*

Butterflies. *Franny's.*

Flying insects and an armadillo. *Franny's.*

Crab and two flying bug pins of gold colored metal enamel and glass by Hattie Carnegie, 1960's. *Muriel Karasik.*

Opposite:
Clear belly fly and earrings of gold washed sterling silver by Trifari. *Jackie Fleischmann.*

Clear belly frog and stork by Trifari, circa 1960. *Bizarre Bazaar.*

Silver frog pavé set with rhinestones. *Maureen McEvoy.*

Flower and gaping fish with colored crystal by Eisenberg, 1940's. *Norman Crider.*

Large sword pin by Jomaz, 1950's. / Lizard pavé set with rhinestones and enameled toes by Coro, 1950's. *Norman Crider.*

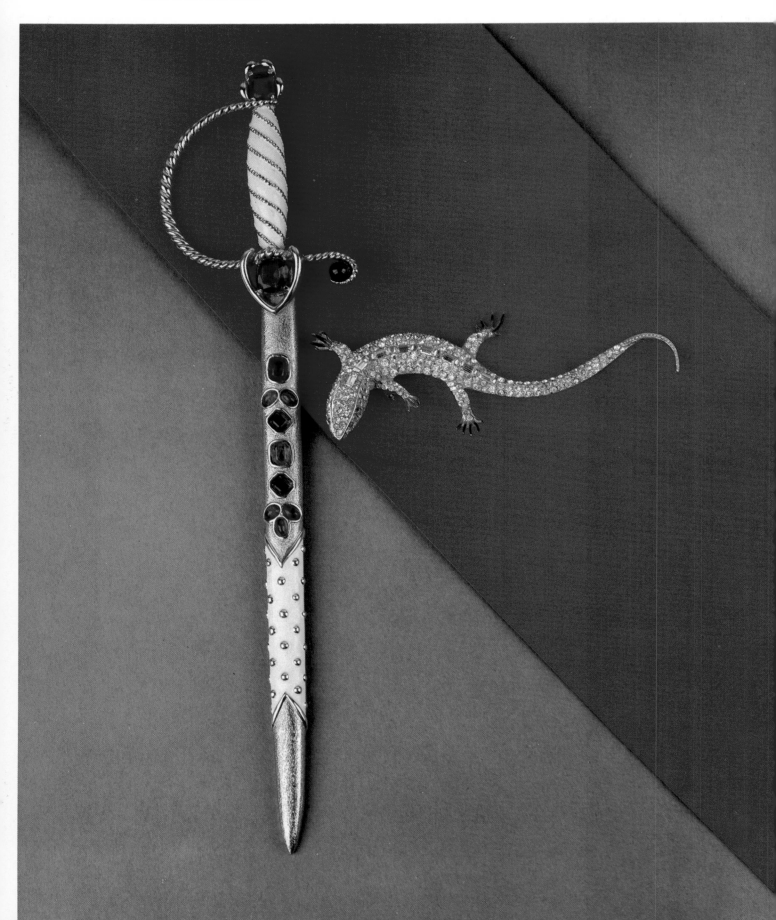

Four pins by Trifari, 1960's. Clear belly frog /
Daggar / Large and small crowns. *Ronnie Seigle.*

Daggar and separate scabbard pin, / King and
Queen of Hearts pin, / Crown and Horse chess-
man by Trifari. *M. Klein.*

King of cards pin by Trifari, 1960's. *Bizarre
Bazaar.*

Enamel pin of woman and wolfhound, 1930's. *Terry Rogers.*

Face of a flapper in ceramic and glaze with rhinestones surrounded by enameled metal figural pins. *Jackie Fleischmann.*

Pin and earrings of molded plastic medallions with rhinestones. *Bob Coyle and Marianne Ward.*

Leather painted pin as head of Josephine Baker with cigarette. *M. Klein.*

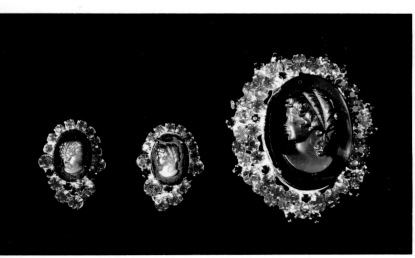

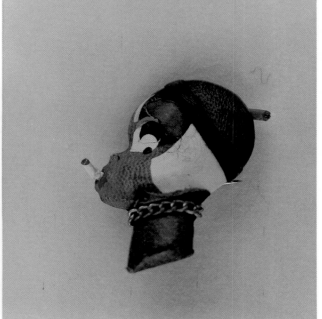

Four blooming mask pins. Three by Mazer including silverface with colored glass diadem and rhinestone hair. / Face pavé set with rhinestones and enameled bow at the side of the neck. / Face pavé set with rhinestones, hair with colored rhinestones. / Silver bow with pendant face and colored stones by Hobé. *Norman Crider.*

Patriotic American insignia by Trifari in the 1940's.

Map of the United States in silver and rhinestones, *Angela Kramer, Inc.*

Silver eagle by Accesscraft, N.Y.C. *Lorraine Matt.*

## Floral Designs

Two fine Italian mosaic work pins in glass. *Franny's.*

Coarse Italian mosaic work. *Rebecca Frey.*

Pin and earrings of iridescent rhinestones. *Jackie Fleischmann.*

Gold washed metal and enameled pins and earrings by Trifari in 1960's.

Floral bouquet in colored wooden beads from Czechoslovakia. *Muriel Karasik.*

Camelia enameled pin by Sarah Coventry, 1950's. *Rebecca Frey.*

Enamel, cabochon glass and rhinestone floral pin by Chanel, 1950's. *Norman Crider.*

White feathers enameled pin by Monet, 1950's. *Rebecca Frey.*

Group of enameled pins and earrings from the 1940's. *Franny's.*

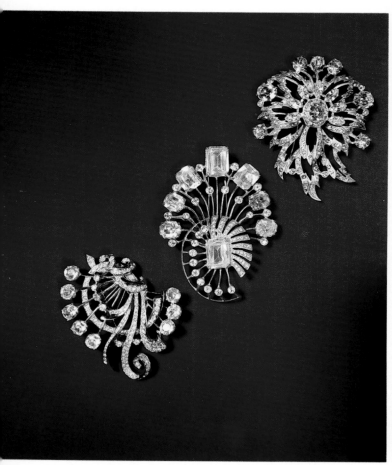

Six crystal and gilt metal pins marked Eisenberg Originals, 1930's. *Norman Crider.*

Egyptian-inspired enamel and rhinestone pin from the 1920's. *Patricia Funt.*

Two sterling silver and crystal floral brooches by Eisenberg, 1940's. *Muriel Karasik.*

Floral sprays (above) and blossom (below) of gold colored metal with rhinestones by Trifari. *Muriel Karasik.*

Bonsai tree of enamel and rhinestone on gold colored metal with unidentified mark, possibly German. *Bizarre Bazaar.*

Three flowers of this design are mounted on springs to tremble when shaken. Pearls, rhinestones and gold colored metal by Hattie Carnegie, 1950's. *Matthew and Michael.*

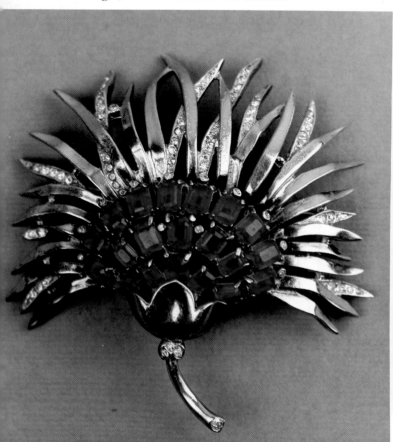

Floral spray of silver with crystal and rhinestones marked Eisenberg Original. 1930's. *Muriel Karasik.*

Enamel and rhinestone blossom by Trifari, 1940's. *Muriel Karasik.*

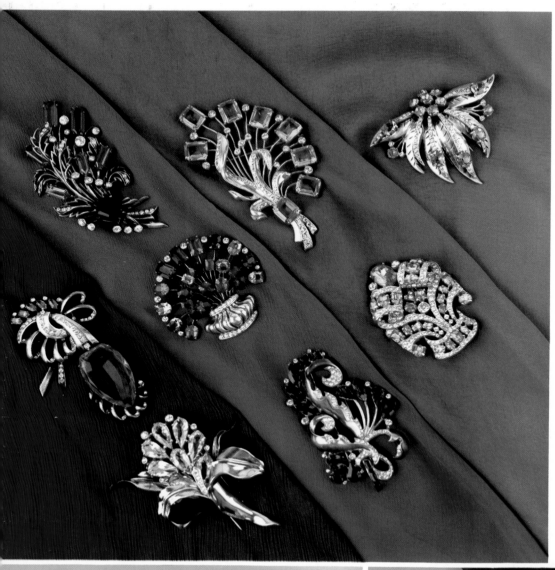

Group of pins by Eisenberg from the 1930's and 1940's. *Norman Crider.*

Plastic stones and gold colored chain mesh as a flower by Miriam Haskell, circa 1940's. *Muriel Karasik.*

Two pins by Hobé. Oval pavé set rhinestones around a colored crystal. Bouquet of sterling silver with colored glass. *Norman Crider.*

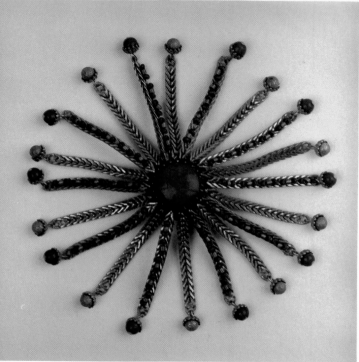

Bracelet of gold colored wire mesh and rhinestones by Boucher. / Pin and earrings of gold washed sterling silver with colored glass and rhinestones in floral design by Pennino, circa 1950. *Norman Crider.*

Pink plastic center with rhinestones and gold colored cast metal flower by Nettie Rosenstein, 1950's. *Terry Rogers.*

Gold washed sterling silver floral pin with rhinestones, unsigned. *Muriel Karasik.*

Iridescent and colored glass grouped around a colorless glass center by Vendome, circa 1955. / Sterling silver wires hold rhinestones in a floral pattern, pin by Vogue, circa 1950. *Norman Crider.*

Bouquet of colored glass and metal wires by Van Dell, 1960's. *Dennis Cogdell.*

Pin and earrings of colored glass, maker unknown, 1950's. *Matthew and Michael.*

Scottish thistle pin and earrings with fancy cut amethyst and cast 9k gold, 1950's. *Franny's.*

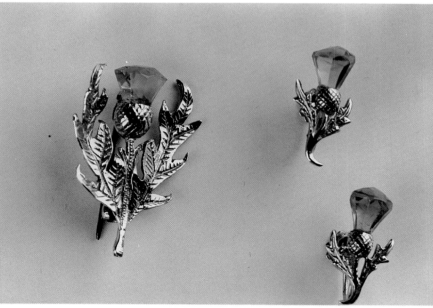

Bouquet in colored glass and pearls by an unknown maker, circa 1950. *Ronnie Seigle.*

Trembling bouquet of pink crystal and silver, unsigned, 1950's. *Jackie Fleischmann.*

Trembling branches of colored glass and rhinestones in the gold washed sterling silver pin with matching earrings, circa 1950. *Ronnie Seigle.*

Round seed pearl and gold metal pin by Miriam Haskell, circa 1940. *Muriel Karasik.*

Three colored glass flowers by Weiss from the 1950's. *Jackie Fleischmann.*

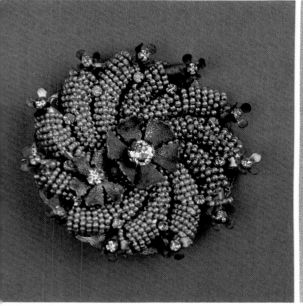

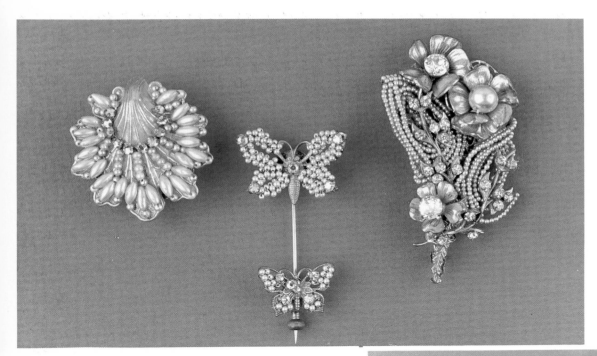

Three pearl, rhinestone and gold colored metal pins by Miriam Haskell, 1940's. *Bizarre Bazaar*

Gold colored metal wheat sheafs in articulated arrangement which bends and moves, by Napier, 1950's. *Marian R. Carroll.*

Plastic beads and cast gold colored metal leaves by Sandor Co., 1950's. *Terry Rogers.*

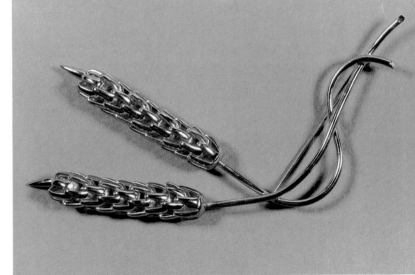

Shells, plastic beads, rhinestones and seed pearls
by Miriam Haskell, circa 1950. *Norman Crider.*

Plastic beads and rhinestones by Miriam Haskell,
circa 1950. *Muriel Karasik.*

Blue glass beads and clear crystal in a domed design, unsigned. *Muriel Karasik.*

Bouquet of colored glass and brass by Joseff of Hollywood, circa 1945. *Muriel Karasik.*

Brass and silver bouquet with colored stones by Harper. *Dennis Cogdell.*

Opposite:
Cast metal and colored rhinestone tree, unsigned. 1950's. *Muriel Karasik.*

Glass, rhinestone and metal blossom by Hattie Carnegie, 1950's. *Terry Rogers.*

Gold and colored glass pin marked Eisenberg Original, 1930's. *Muriel Karasik.*

Gold washed silver and colored glass man holding cornucopia and flowers marked Eisenberg Original, 1930's. *Muriel Karasik.*

### Non-floral Designs

Pin and earrings of silver with rhinestones in an imitation of Art Deco style
by Sarah Coventry circa 1955. *Ann's
Arts.*

Silver and rhinestone pin of authentic
Art Deco style, unsigned, circa 1925.
*Muriel Karasik.*

Opposite:
Clip of clear and colored rhinestones by
Eisenberg, 1940's. *Angela Kramer, Inc.*

Three clips of rhinestones. The rounded
clips have interchangeable color bars
imitating coral and onyx, unsigned,
1940's. *Bizarre Bazaar.*

Double clip brooch of rhinestones that
separates into two matching clips,
unsigned, circa 1950. *Matthew and
Michael.*

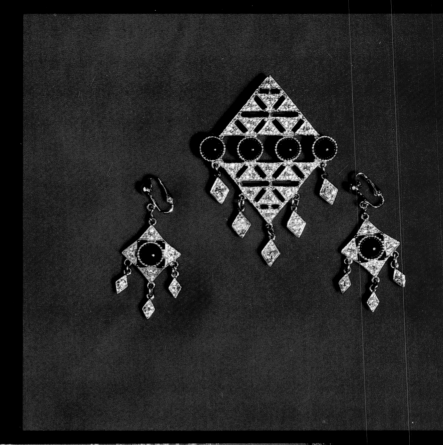

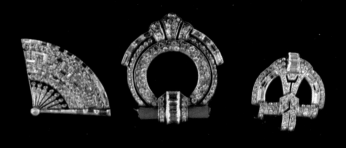

Pin pave set with rhinestones including baguettes, by Kramer. New York, 1950's. *Marian R. Carroll.*

Pin in Art Deco style pavé set with colored and clear rhinestones, unsigned, circa 1955. *Matthew and Michael.*

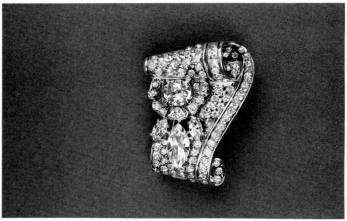

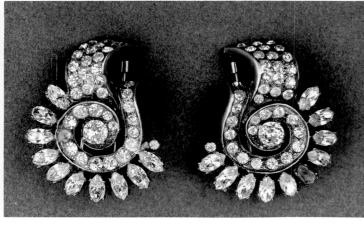

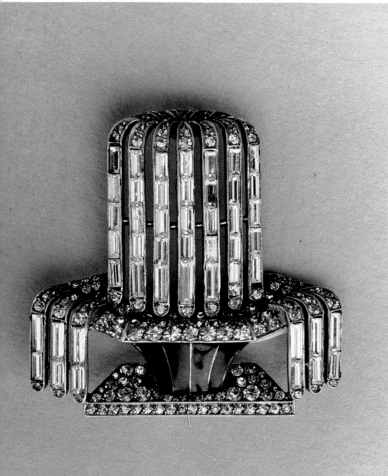

Three crystal and rhinestone clips of sterling silver by Eisenberg, circa 1940. *Muriel Karasik.*

Silver, rhinestone and enameled fountain in Art Deco style, 1930's. *Maureen McEvoy.*

Triangular pin of rhinestones and false pearls, unsigned, *Terry Rogers.*

Colored and clear foiled glass bar pin from the 1930's, unsigned. *Jackie Fleischmann.*

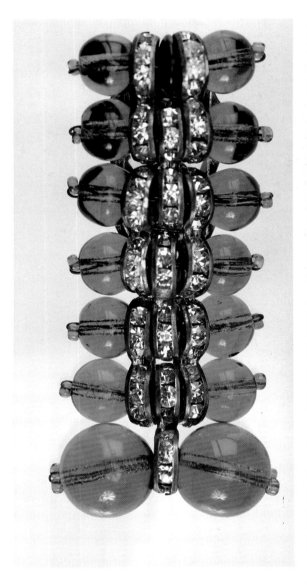

Silver and glass pin in the form of clock hands by Boucher, 1950's. *Bizarre Bazaar.*

Silver double jabot pin pavé set with rhinestones, circa 1925. *Maureen McEvoy.*

Crystal and rhinestone clip signed Eisenberg Original, 1940's. *Jackie Fleischmann.*

Colored glass and rhinestone clip, 1940's. *Jackie Fleischmann.*

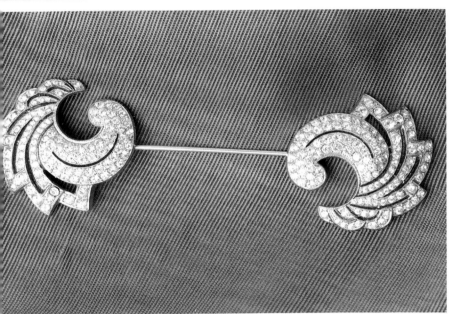

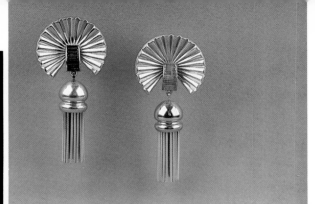

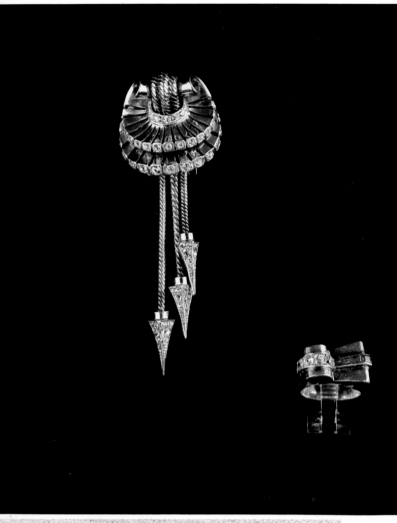

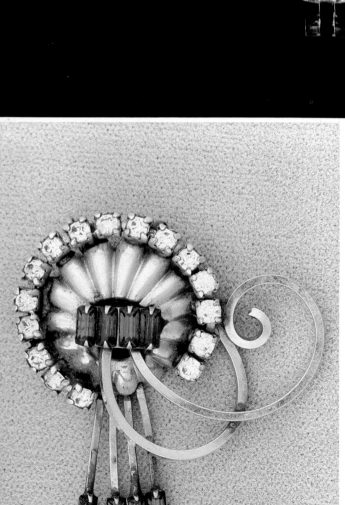

Clip with tassel drops and ring of gold washed silver with rhinestones, French, 1940's. *Bizarre Bazaar.*

Pair of clips with tassel drops and colored rhinestones, 1940's. *Bizarre Bazaar.*

Clip with pierced fan and tassel drops with rhinestones, 1940's, *Bizarre Bazaar.*

Pin with scrolled cone and collar of colored glass and rhinestones by Reja, 1940's. *Bizarre Bazaar.*

Pin with colored glass and rhinestones by Beal-Ron, 1940's. *Dennis Cogdell.*

Colored glass and rhinestone pin, unsigned, 1950's. *Rebecca Frey.*

Round swirl pin with rhinestones, unsigned, 1950's. *Rebecca Frey.*

Two colored glass and cast metal pins from the 1950's. Left signed François. / Right signed Art. *Franny's.*

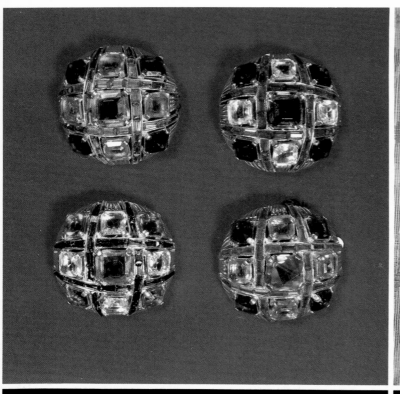

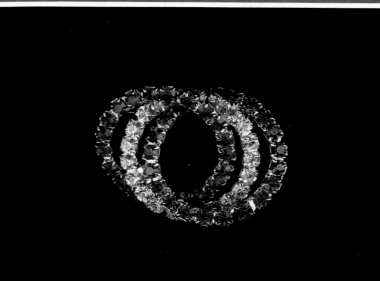

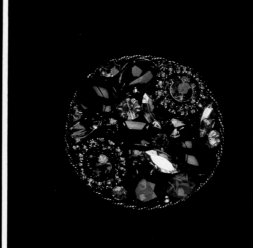

Four pins with colored glass set in cast gold washed metal by Boucher, circa 1960. *Norman Crider.*

Pin and earrings with brown, opaline and clear colored glass by Schiaparelli, 1950's. *Muriel Karasik.*

Three linked circles in colored rhinestones, unsigned, circa 1950. *Rebecca Frey.*

Brown and iridescent stones of various shapes grouped together in a circle by Weiss, 1950's. *Lorraine Matt.*

Triangular pin set with yellow rhinestones made by Kramer for Dior, circa 1950. *Matthew and Michael.*

Colored glass in cabochon and facet cuts with silver, by Trifari, 1950's. *M. Klein.*

Oval dome pavé set with cabuchon and facet cut colored glass by Schreiner, New York, *Matthew and Michael.*

Black enameled metal wire with colored glass in a domed shape, unsigned, 1960's. *Matthew and Michael.*

Cabochon colored glass and rhinestones in silver setting by Di Nicola, 1960's. *Matthew and Michael.*

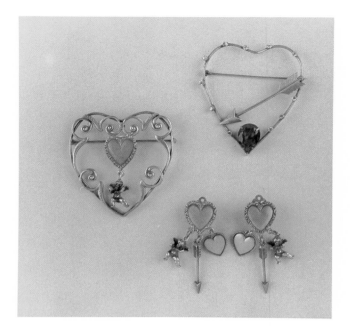

Two pins and earrings of brass wire heart motifs by Joseff of Hollywood, circa 1945. *M. Klein.*

Two gold washed sterling silver pins with colored crystals by Hobé, circa 1915. *M. Klein.*

Opposite and this page:
Necklace and thirteen pins of
sterling silver with colored
crystals, circa 1920 by Hobé.
*Norman Crider.*

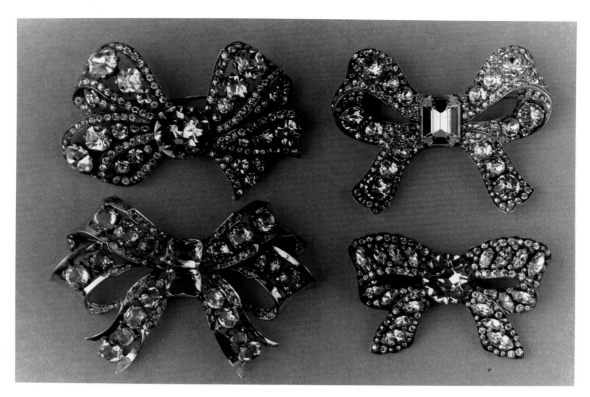

Four crystal and sterling silver bow-shaped pins signed Eisenberg Original, 1940's. *Bizarre Bazaar.*

Gold washed silver pin with green crystals signed Eisenberg Original, 1930's. *Muriel Karasik.*

Bow pin of gold washed sterling silver with clear and colored glass by Vogue. / Bow pin of silver colored metal with enamel and rhinestones by Chanel. *Ronnie Seigle.*

Five pins with rhinestones and false pearls by Kenneth J. Lane, 1970-1985.

Crystal and rhinestones in sterling silver marked Eisenberg Original, 1940's. *Muriel Karasik.*

Sterling silver, rhinestone and pearl pin, unsigned. *Linda Morgan.*

Two rhinestone and sterling silver pins marked Eisenberg Originals, circa 1935-1945. *Bizarre Bazaar.*

Gold washed metal mesh bow pin by Vendome, 1940's. / Rhinestone and blue glass bow pin, unsigned, 1940's. *Bizarre Bazaar.*

Blue baguette glass in yellow metal setting by Danecraft, 1950's. *Matthew and Michael.*

Circle pin with bow in baguettes and rhinestones, unmarked, 1950's. *Rebecca Frey.*

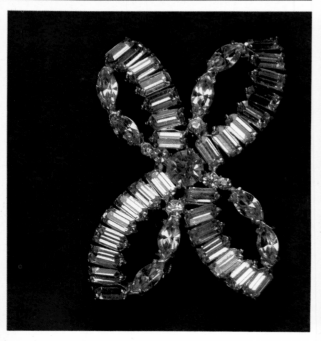

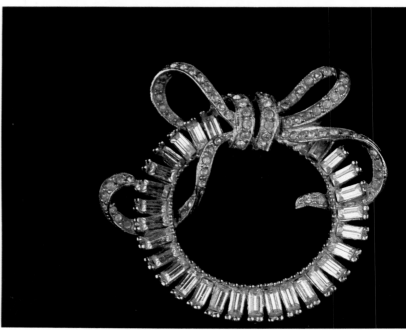

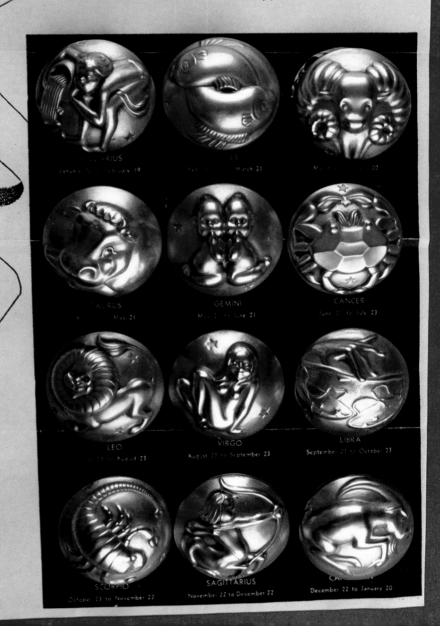

Rhinestone and yellow metal star pin by Tanger, 1950's. *Terry Rogers.*

Star burst of brown glass and burnished cast metal by Schiaparelli, 1940's. *Terry Rogers.*

Twelve relief medallions of the signs of the zodiac in brass with a gold finish by Joseff of Hollywood, circa 1945. *M. Klein.*

Exclusive with John Wanamaker, New York . . . Signatures of the stars, whimsical signs of the Zodiac wrought by a skilled craftsman.

14Kt gold pin                Matching 14Kt. gold earrings,  Pair
Sterling silver pin            Matching sterling silver earrings, Pair

Fine Jewelry\*, Street Floor.

English paste-set earrings of silver, mid-nineteenth century. *Maureen McEvoy.*

English paste and pearl set earrings of silver, circa 1905, *Maureen McEvoy.*

Silver and paste earrings, probably French, late nineteenth century. / Brooch of colored glass and rhinestones, circa 1920. / Necklace of silver, emerald paste and rhinestones, circa 1910. *Patricia Funt.*

# Earrings

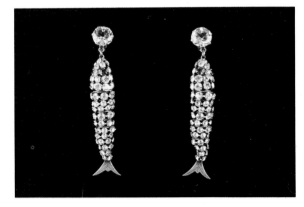

Silver and rhinestone earrings, circa 1955. *Marian R. Carroll.*

Silver and rhinestone earrings, copies of a late nineteenth century style, circa 1950. *M. Klein.*

French paste earrings from the 1920's. *Michael Greenberg.*

French paste earrings as articulated fish, late nineteenth century. *Angela Kramer, Inc.*

Silver, rhinestones and papier-maché false Baroque pearls as drop earrings, unsigned, circa 1910. *Maureen McEvoy.*

Silver openwork drop earrings with blue and clear rhinestones, circa 1920. *M. Klein.*

Markasite and green glass drop earrings from the 1920's. *Bizarre Bazaar.*

Moulded cameos in silver rope collet on ear wires. Circa 1930's. *M. Klein.*

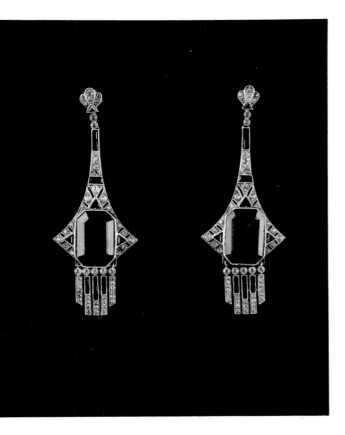

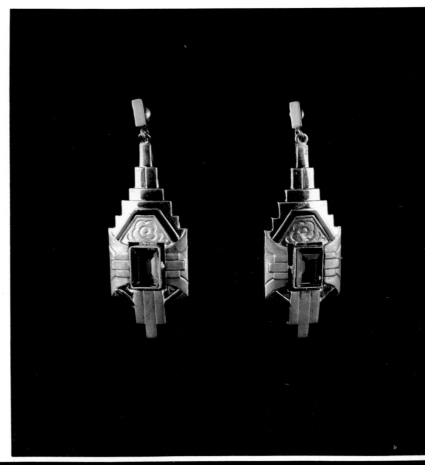

French, 935 silver drop earrings with green paste, circa 1915. *Angela Kramer, Inc.*

German silver and colored glass drop earrings from the 1920's. *Angela Kramer, Inc.*

Two pair of German silver, rhinestone and colored glass drop earrings from the 1920's. *Bizarre Bazaar.*

Cast gold colored metal and pearl drop earrings reflecting a Renaissance revival influence by Joseff of Hollywood, circa 1945. *M. Klein.*

Silver and dark pink glass dangle earrings from 1960's. / Red glass and rhinestone earclips by Trifari, 1960's. / Silver and pavé rhinestones in clip earrings by Schiaparelli, circa 1950. *M. Klein.*

Colored glass earrings from the 1950's. *Jackie Fleischmann.*

Opposite:

Purple glass and rhinestone earrings, 1950's. *Jackie Fleischmann.*

Carved opaque glass and colored rhinestones as a pin and earrings, 1950's. *Franny's.*

Clip earrings of red cabochons and clear rhinestones by Mazer, 1960's. *Terry Rogers.*

Colored glass and rhinestones by Polcini, circa 1960. *Terry Rogers.*

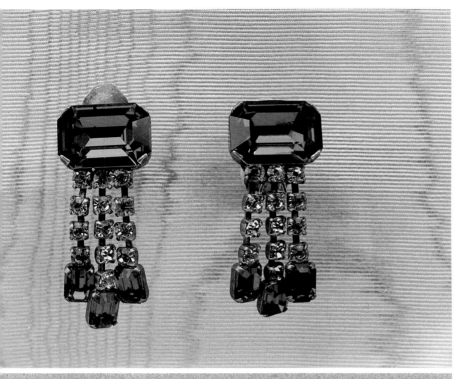

Pin and six pair of earrings with clear silver foil backed crystal featured as the main element of the design, by Kenneth J. Lane, circa 1970.

Three sets of pin and earrings by an unknown maker including iridescent and colored glass in gold metal, 1950's. *Franny's.*

Rhinestones and false pearl drop earrings, 1960's. *Matthew and Michael.*

Colored glass and rhinestone ear clips, 1960's. *Matthew and Michael.*

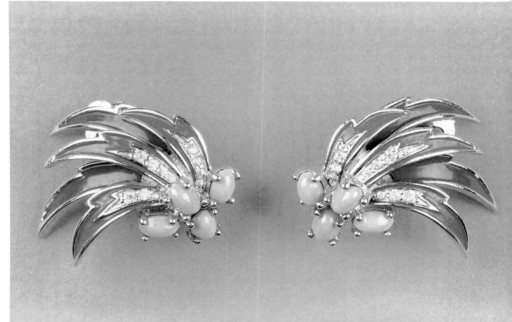

Earrings with plastic ivory face in gold metal setting with green and iridescent stones by H.A.R. *Ronnie Seigle.*

Aqua glass and rhinestone earrings by Trifari, circa 1960. / Enamel and rhinestone earrings shaped as women's shoes, circa 1950. *M. Klein.*

Enameled metal and pink opaque stones by Mazer, circa 1960. *Terry Rogers.*

Coral colored plastic and rhinestones as a coiled worm, unmarked. / Pin and earrings with false pearl, turquoise colored plastic and rhinestones in gold colored metal by Ciner, circa 1950. *M. Klein.*

Two pair of false pearl and rhinestone dangle earrings by Miriam Haskell, circa 1955. *Bizarre Bazaar.*

Colored glass and rhinestone drop earrings by Kenneth J. Lane, circa 1970. *Marian R. Carroll.*

Silver colored metal and black plastic ear covers with clips at the bottom and top from Sarah Coventry, 1960's. *Terry Rogers.*

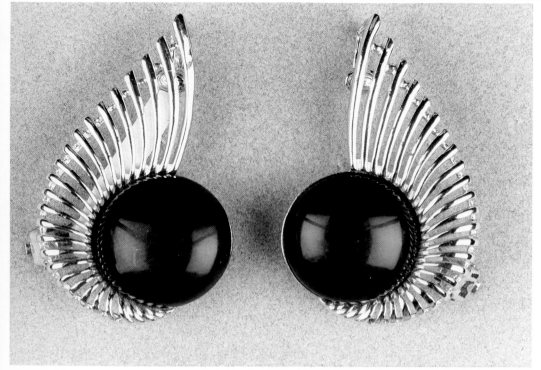

Five pair of earrings by Kenneth J. Lane from the mid-1960's. The orange pave set drop style is among his earliest designs.

Ten pair of earrings by Kenneth J. Lane from the 1970's. Fine colored crystal stones are included.

Pearl imitations featured as the main design element in earrings with bracelet and necklaces by Trifari, 1970's.

Opposite:
Seven pair of earrings featuring false pearls in dynamic designs from the 1970's by Kenneth J. Lane.

Pin and earrings featuring bold designs in enameled metal from the 1980's by Kenneth J. Lane.

# *Bibliography*

Baker, Lillian. *Art Nouveau and Art Deco Jewelry*, Paducah, KY: Collector Books, no date.
_____ *Fifty Years of Collectible Fashion Jewelry 1925-1975*, Paducah, KY: Collector Books, 1986.
Becker, Vivienne, *Antique and 20th Century Jewerly*, London: N.A.G. Press, 1980.
_____ *Art Nouveau Jewelry*, London: Thames and Hudson, 1985.
Bell, Jeanenne, *Answers to Questions About Old Jewelry, 1840 to 1950*, 2nd Edition, Florence, AL: Books Americana Inc., 1985.
Bury, Shirley, *Jewellery Gallery Summary Catalog*, London: Victoria and Albert Museum, 1982.
Darling, Ada, *Antique Jewelry*, Watkins Glen, NY: Century House, 1953.
Dolan, Maryanne, *An Identification and Value Guide to Collecting Rhinestone Jewelry*, Florence, AL: Books Americana Inc., 1984.
Hughes, Graham, *The Art of Jewelry, A Survey of Craft and Creation*, NY: Gallery Books, W.H. Smith Publishers, 1984.
Lewis, M.D.S., *Antique Paste Jewellery*, London: Faber and Faber, 1970.
Lynnlee, J.L., *All That Glitters*, West Chester, PA: Schiffer, 1986.
Newman, Harold, *An Illustrated Dictionary of Jewelry*, London: Thames and Hudson, 1981.
Poynder, Michael, *The Price Guide to Jewellery, 3000 B.C. - 1950 A.D.*, Woodbridge, Suffolk: Antique Collector's Club, 1976.
Raulet, Sylvie, *Art Deco Jewelry*, London: Thames and Hudson, 1985.
Rothstein, Natalie, ed., *Four Hundred Years of Fashion*, London: Victoria and Albert Museum in association with William Collins, 1984.
Sataloff, Joseph, *Art Nouveau Jewelry*, Bryn Mawr, PA: Dorrance & Company, 1984.
Scarisbrick, Diane, *Jewellery*, London: B.T. Batsford Ltd., 1984.
Tait, Hugh, ed., *Seven Thousand Years of Jewellery*, London: British Museum, 1986.

# Index

# Price Guide

Values vary immensely according to an article's condition, location of the market, parts of the country, and overall quality of design. While one must make their own decisions, we can offer a guide.

| | | | | | | |
|---|---|---|---|---|---|
| Title page. Necklace | 125-150 | p-26. Necklace and | | p-46. 3 Necklaces | 75-95 each |
| Bracelet and | | earrings | 350-550 | Collar | 125-200 |
| earrings | 150-200 | Parure | 325-375 | earrings | 35-55 |
| Earrings | 75-95 | p-27. Parure | 1200-1400 | p-47. Necklace | 1500-up |
| Necklace | 250-275 | p-28. Choker, English | 350-450 | p-48. Collar | 300-395 |
| p-4. Star, *Memento* | 125-200 | Necklace | 400-500 | Collar, Lane | 1500-up |
| Star | 125-200 | Choker, French | 400-500 | p-49. Collar and | |
| p-5. Brooch | 250-up | p-29. Choker | 400-475 | earrings | 750-800 |
| p-8. Ring | 175-200 | p-30. Choker, wooden | 125-200 | Collar | 250-350 |
| Earrings, silver | 150-200 | Choker and earrings | 120-175 | Collar and earrings | 250-350 |
| Pinchbeck earrings | 100-150 | Choker, Roman | 250-325 | p-50. Collar | 1500-up |
| Two pair Pinchbeck | | p-31. Choker | 45-85 | p-51. Collar, brown | 95-150 |
| earrings | 100-150 a pair | Clips | 60-80 | Collar, red | 325-400 |
| Alloy earrings | 100-150 | Pin | 50-65 | p-52. Collar | 125-200 |
| p-9. Necklace, English | 125-175 | p-32. Choker, wooden | 125-200 | Collar, Lane | 300-500 |
| Necklace, English | 125-175 | Choker, Haskell | 400-485 | p-53. Collar, blue | 150-200 |
| Pin | 100-125 | p-33. Choker | 350-400 | Collar | 600-700 |
| Pinchbeck necklace | 525-600 | p-34. Choker, Civer | 450-525 | p-54. Necklace, Japan | 55-95 |
| Edwardian pendant | 100-125 | Choker, Boucher | 300-350 | Necklace, black | 125-200 |
| p-10. Clear fin Marlin | 175-225 | p-35. Choker and | | Necklace, clear and | |
| Small peach fish | 40-55 | earrings , Lane | 250-300 | black | 65-100 |
| Beige swordfish | 75-100 | p-36. Choker and | | Necklace, wired | 75-110 |
| Round red fish | 135-175 | earrings | 175-250 | Necklace, silver and | |
| Red swordfish | 100-125 | Choker | 150-195 | black | 80-120 |
| Lobster | 175-225 | Earrings | 125-175 | Necklace, glass | 85-120 |
| Black and white fish | 75-100 | p-37. Necklace | 300-385 | Necklace, wooden | 120-150 |
| Clear and red fish | 85-125 | Necklace, Bakelite | 85-125 | p-55. Necklace and | |
| Seashell clip | 45-65 | Necklace, Classical | 75-100 | bracelet | 225-275 |
| Green fish | 75-100 | Choker and earrings | 150-200 | Choker, Venetian | 125-200 |
| p-11. Carved bracelet | 75-125 | p-38. Necklace, pin- | | Choker | 85-120 |
| Beads bracelet | 85-100 | netta | 350-400 | Necklace | 85-120 |
| p-13. Long necklace | 45-65 | Necklace and | | p-56. Necklace and | |
| Earrings, triangular | 25-35 | bracelet | 250-325 | earrings | 600-750 |
| Short necklace | 65-85 | Necklace, Phyllis, | | p-57. Necklace | 75-100 |
| Earrings | 25-35 | sterling | 150-175 | Earrings, necklace | |
| Bracelet | 45-65 | p-39. Necklace and | | and bracelet | 150-225 |
| p-15. Pendant | 65-75 | earrings | 165-200 | Choker | 75-100 |
| Bangle bracelet | 65-85 | Choker and earrings | 130-170 | Necklace | 95-125 |
| Earrings | 25-45 | Choker and | | p-58. Necklace, white | |
| Link bracelet | 45-65 | earrings, | | glass | 125-200 |
| Pearl necklace | 85-95 | Eisenberg Ice | 375-450 | Necklace, ceramic | 125-200 |
| Pin | 35-45 | Necklace and | | Necklace, clear | 125-200 |
| Earrings | 25-35 | earrings | 275-300 | p-59. Necklace, glass | 125-145 |
| p-16. Parure | 1800-up | p-40. Necklace | 200-250 | Necklace, wood | 50-95 |
| p-17. Parure | 1500-1800 | Choker | 250-300 | Necklace, ceramic | 125-145 |
| p-18. Parure | 750-900 | p-41. Choker | 95-115 | p-60. Necklace and | |
| p-19. Parure, Harper | 55-95 | Necklace and | | earrings | 200-250 |
| Parure, Trifari | 300-400 | earrings | 530-600 | Choker | 125-150 |
| Large crown | 150-175 | p-42. Necklace | 85-120 | Necklace and | |
| Small crown | 90-110 | Necklace and | | earrings, Monet | 125-150 |
| p-20. Parure | 750-950 | earrings | 700-775 | p-61. Necklace, opera | 250-300 |
| p-21. Parure | 800-1000 | p-43. Necklace | 450-500 | Necklace, short | 240-275 |
| p-22. Parure | 250-300 | Necklace and | | Choker | 675-700 |
| p-23. Parure, Hobé | 95-125 | earrings, blue | 200-250 | p-62. Necklace, opera | 1200-1500 |
| Parure, Coventry | 50-95 | Necklace and | | Two chokers | 250-350 (each) |
| Parure, Matisse | 125-145 | earrings, purple | 75-125 | Necklace and | |
| p-24. Parure, Kramer | 200-300 | p-44. Necklace and | | earrings | 175-225 |
| Parure | 250-325 | earrings | 700-800 | p-63. Necklace, short, | |
| p-25. Parure | 850-1000 | p-45. Necklace | 600-700 | earrings  bracelet | 85-110 |

| | |
|---|---|
| Necklace, long | 45-65 |
| Necklace, medium | 35-55 |
| Twisted bracelet, earrings and pin | 65-85 |
| Twisted necklace and bracelet | 85-100 |
| Pendant and earrings, floral | 35-45 |
| Pendant and earrings, leaves | 35-45 |
| Pendant and earrings, diamonds | 35-45 |
| Choker | 350-500 |
| p-64. Pendant and bracelet | 195-250 |
| Pendant, brass | 75-125 |
| Pendant, black | 175-200 |
| p-65. Pendant, Carnegie | 150-200 |
| Pendant, Lane | 125-195 |
| Pendant, leaf | 35-50 |
| Pendant and earrings, shell | 70-90 |
| Necklace and earrings, leaves | 65-85 |
| Pendant, long leaf | 35-55 |
| Pendant, pin and earrings, single leaf | 50-70 |
| Pendant, pin and earrings, leaf group | 75-95 |
| p-66. Necklace | 175-225 |
| Choker | 110-150 |
| p-67. Pendant, square | 85-100 |
| Pendant, coin | 75-95 |
| Pin | 60-85 |
| Earrings and pendant | 200-250 |
| Pendant necklace | 125-180 |
| p-68. Pendant, Renaissance | 500-575 |
| Pin and earrings | 75-95 |
| Pendant, glass | 50-75 |
| p-69. Pendant and earrings | 100-150 |
| Pendant | 50-75 |
| Pendant and earrings, Austrian | 75-95 |
| p-70. Pendant | 150-200 |
| p-71. Pendant, jade | 350-500 |
| Pendant, Lane | 300-500 |
| p-72. Pendant, Art Nouveau | 95-150 |
| Pendant, Haskell | 800-900 |
| p-73. Pendant | 525-700 |
| p-74. Pendant | 300-350 |
| p-75. Pendant, Schiaparelli | 425-500 |
| Pendant, Haskell | 350-450 |
| p-76. Pendant | 450-550 |
| p-77. Pendant, Hobé | 575-650 |
| Pendant, Austria | 500-650 |
| p-78. Pendant | 300-385 |
| p-79. Pendant, 2 drops | 95-125 |
| Pendant and earrings | 100-150 |
| Pendant, briolette | 200-225 |

| | |
|---|---|
| Pendant, colored | 150-175 |
| p-80. Pendant, Baroque | 100-175 |
| Pendant, beads | 195-250 |
| p-81. Pendant | 110-185 |
| p-82. Pendant | 500-600 |
| p-83. Bracelet | 450-550 |
| Bracelet | 450-550 |
| p-84. Bracelet | special |
| p-85. Link bracelet, Eisenberg Ice | 400-500 |
| Bracelet, expansion | 450-500 |
| Link bracelet, French | 450-550 |
| Link bracelet, Robért | 400-450 |
| p-86. Brooch | 250-300 |
| Link bracelet | 395-450 |
| Pin | 95-175 |
| Link bracelet, Cartier style | 200-275 |
| Seven link bracelet | 200-275 |
| Articulated link bracelet | 200-275 |
| Link bracelet, Art Deco | 400-450 |
| p-87. Link bracelet | 125-175 |
| Link bracelet, Art Deco | 475-575 |
| Articulated link bracelet | 450-500 |
| p-88. Link bracelet, French | 375-450 |
| Link bracelet | 400-450 |
| p-89. Link bracelet, Schiaparelli | 395-480 |
| Link bracelet, gold | 600-650 |
| Link bracelet, rhinestones (by Trifari) | 150-175 |
| p-90. Link braclet | 350-400 |
| Brooch | 750-1200 |
| Link bracelet, yellow | 750-900 |
| Link bracelet, clear and blue | 775-850 |
| Link bracelet, blue | 700-800 |
| p-91. Brooch | 750-895 |
| Link bracelet, Hobé | 1800-2000 |
| Link bracelet and brooch | 750-900 |
| p-92. Link bracelet, mesh | 200-250 |
| Link bracelet, Ciner | 195-250 |
| Link bracelet, Eton | 225-295 |
| Link bracelet, silver | 450-550 |
| Link bracelet, S. Boucher | 350-500 |
| p-93. Link bracelet, Eisenberg Ice | 150-200 |
| Link bracelet, yellow | 250-350 |
| Link bracelet, Victorian | 200-275 |
| Link bracelet, medallions | 50-95 |
| p-94. Pin and link bracelet, sterling | 175-250 |
| Pin, wagon | 145-170 |
| Pin, thimble | 95-120 |
| Link bracelet | 250-400 |
| p-95. Link bracelet, glass | 275-350 |
| Link bracelet, metal | 270-290 |

| | |
|---|---|
| p-96. Link bracelet | 500-575 |
| Four link bracelets, mosaics | 45-75 |
| Link bracelet, scarabs | 55-75 |
| p-97. Bar pin | 65-95 |
| Pendant, real beetle | 75-100 |
| Bangle bracelet | 68-95 |
| Pendant, stone | 78-120 |
| Bracelet, large stones | 145-200 |
| Bracelet, small stones | 75-150 |
| Silver link bracelet | 65-125 |
| Silver link bracelet, 6 large | 35-60 |
| Pin | 30-50 |
| Earrings | 25-40 |
| Silver link bracelet, 6 small | 35-50 |
| Bracelet, 6 on double links | 35-50 |
| p-98. Bangle bracelet and earrings | 175-300 |
| Pearl bracelet | 65-100 |
| Bangle bracelet | 400-450 |
| p-99. Bracelet, wooden | 120-150 |
| Bangle bracelet | 650-700 |
| Hinged bracelet | 125-145 |
| p-100. Bangle bracelet, shake | 125-200 |
| Bangle bracelet, horse | 125-200 |
| Bracelet, pink stones | 95-150 |
| Clear bracelet | 125-up |
| Black enamel bracelet | 140-175 |
| Ring, snake | 125-150 |
| p-101. Zebra heads bracelet | 200-250 |
| Bracelet and earrings, brown | 200-250 |
| Coral bracelet | 125-200 |
| Red & Green braclet | 125-200 |
| Ring, silver | 125-150 |
| Hinged bracelet, Lane | 125-200 |
| Hinged bracelet, Jomaz | 125-200 |
| p-102. Bracelet, black and white | 75-95 |
| Bracelet, animal heads | 95-120 |
| Bracelet, white and brown | 65-90 |
| Bracelet, buckle | 75-90 |
| Bracelet, tiger eye | 90-110 |
| Bracelet, red and black | 120-150 |
| Bracelet, gold | 125-150 |
| Bracelet, shell | 100-125 |
| Bracelet, silver | 95-120 |
| Bracelet, turquoise | 95-125 |
| p-103. Small plane pin | 25-40 |
| Large plane pin | 35-50 |
| Ship pin, Damascene | 25-40 |
| Dog pin | 35-50 |
| Bob-cat pin | 95-125 |
| p-104. Flying eagle pin | 125-175 |

| | |
|---|---|
| Small eagle pin | 95-120 |
| Duck pin | 120-150 |
| Fish pin | 125-175 |
| Swan pin | 175-225 |
| Rooster pin | 175-225 |
| Flower pin | 95-120 |
| p-105. Bird pin | 400-450 |
| Ostrich pin | 125-175 |
| Pigeon pin, sterling | 75-95 |
| Blue bird pin | 35-55 |
| Gold bird pin | 35-55 |
| Red bird pin | 25-45 |
| p-106. Owl pin on coral | 25-35 |
| Silver owl pin | 25-35 |
| Green owl pin | 35-45 |
| Gold owl pin | 25-35 |
| Rhinestone owl pin | 25-35 |
| Imaginary bird pin, rhinestones | 50-65 |
| Sterling, 3 birds and branch pin | 60-75 |
| Peacock pin, blue | 40-75 |
| Blue and yellow bird pin | 75-95 |
| Light blue and silver bird pin | 60-75 |
| Two birds pin | 35-55 |
| Rhinestone bird pin | 35-55 |
| Tie bar, sterling | 30-50 |
| Pearl swan pin | 35-55 |
| Gold swan pin | 30-50 |
| p-107. Sterling cat pin by Beau | 25-40 |
| Blue cat pin | 15-25 |
| Two cat pins | 15-25 |
| Mouse pin | 15-25 |
| Crop and horsehead pin | 20-30 |
| Reverse carved crystal pin | 35-50 |
| Horse head charm | 20-30 |
| Crop and cap pin | 35-50 |
| Two pins and earrings | 150-200 |
| Silver horse head pin | 15-35 |
| Brown horse pin | 15-35 |
| Gold horse head pin | 25-40 |
| Earrings | 25-35 |
| Gold running horse pin | 25-40 |
| Silver running horse pin | 30-40 |
| Donkey pin | 15-25 |
| p-108. Silver greyhounds racing pins: | |
| Two dogs | 50-65 |
| Three dogs | 75-95 |
| Rhinestones | 45-70 |
| #7 and rhine- stones | 75-95 |
| Wooden puppy pin | 15-25 |
| Two metal dogs pin | 30-45 |
| Black scotty pin, plastic | 45-55 |
| Single Dachshund pin | 15-25 |
| Wooden dog pin | 20-40 |
| Double dachshund pin | 25-40 |

| | |
|---|---|
| White Celluloid scotty pin | 45-65 |
| Two Bakelite scotties pin | 65-75 |
| Silver dog charm | 45-60 |
| Rhinestone dachs- hund pin | 20-30 |
| Double rhinestone scotties pin | 20-30 |
| Gold rhinestone scotties pin | 15-25 |
| Silver rhinestone scotties pin | 15-25 |
| p-109. Elephants: | |
| Rhinestone full body pin | 350-375 |
| Copper pin by Kim | 65-75 |
| Rhinestone face pin | 150-200 |
| Red leather pin | 95-120 |
| Green crystals, full body pin | 65-80 |
| Green Bakelite pin | 400-450 |
| Gold with black glasses pin | 50-70 |
| Grey plastic head and Bakelite body rattle | 190-220 |
| Red jacket by MMC | 50-75 |
| Red full body pin | 50-75 |
| Sterling and rhine- stone elephant pin | 125-150 |
| Fish with chains pin | 300-350 |
| Dog with chains pin | 300-350 |
| Tiger pin | 30-50 |
| Gold elephant pin | 25-50 |
| p-110. Two monkeys pin | 125-175 |
| Bird pin | 100-150 |
| Dragonfly pin | 125-165 |
| Snake pin | 125-150 |
| Large bird pin | 85-150 |
| Crocodile pin | 150-200 |
| Dragonfly pin | 75-95 |
| Snail pin | 90-110 |
| Bird pin | 75-100 |
| p-111. Butterfly pin | 40-75 |
| Dragonfly pin | 300-395 |
| p-112. Butterfly pins: | |
| Silver filigree | 15-30 |
| Enameled wings | 15-25 |
| Mother-of-Pearl wings | 20-40 |
| Japanese gold and enamel | 35-50 |
| Silver pierced wings | 25-35 |
| Rhinestone and pearl wings | 25-40 |
| Gold wings | 15-30 |
| Filigree gold wings | 20-40 |
| Rhinestone and enamel wings | 20-40 |
| Enamel wings | 15-25 |
| Pierced and rhine- stone wings | 35-45 |
| Dragonfly with mother-of-pearl | 30-45 |

| | |
|---|---|
| Flying insects pins: | |
| Praying mantis | 15-30 |
| White bee | 20-40 |
| Black fly | 15-35 |
| Japanese black bee | 25-45 |
| Scarab beetle | 30-50 |
| Armadillo | 15-25 |
| Gold and stone bee | 28-40 |
| Silver dragonfly | 30-45 |
| Crab pin | 90-110 |
| Green bug pin | 75-95 |
| Pink bug pin | 75-95 |
| p-113. Fly pin and earrings | 150-200 |
| Frog pin | 200-225 |
| Stork pin | 200-225 |
| Pavé frog pin | 150-200 |
| Flower pin | 650-725 |
| Fish pin | 550-625 |
| p-114. Sword pin | 550-600 |
| Lizard pin | 350-450 |
| p-115. Frog pin | 200-225 |
| Daggar pin | 75-100 |
| Large crown | 150-175 |
| Small crown | 90-110 |
| Daggar in scabbard pin | 325-400 |
| King and Queen pins | 80-110 |
| Crown pin | 150-175 |
| Chess man pin | 90-125 |
| King of cards pin | 150-195 |
| p-116. Enamel pin | 75-100 |
| Flapper pin | 40-75 |
| Bird pin, plastic, 1930's | 35-50 |
| Blue racoon pin | 40-60 |
| Deer pin by Boucher | 50-70 |
| Fish pin | 50-70 |
| Worm pin | 40-60 |
| Pin and earrings | 65-95 |
| Leather pin | 75-100 |
| p-117. Silverface pin | 850-900 |
| Face pin with bow | 550-600 |
| Face pin with colored stones | 450-500 |
| Bow and face pin | 1200-1250 |
| p-118. Three bracelets | 45-75 each |
| Ten patriotic pins | 45-75 each |
| Map pin | 150-250 |
| Eagle pin | 45-75 |
| p-119. Mosaic pin, bird | 85-100 |
| Mosaic pin, daisies | 85-100 |
| Mosaic pin, blue circle | 25-45 |
| Pin and earrings | 125-150 |
| p-120. Earrings and two pins, blue | 65-80 |
| Rose pin | 35-50 |
| Wing earrings | 25-40 |
| Earrings and pin, turquuoise | 45-60 |
| Small bird pin | 35-50 |
| Large bird pin | 65-80 |
| Floral pin, wooden | 90-110 |
| Camelia pin | 25-45 |
| p-121. Enamel pin | 150-175 |
| White feathers pin | 25-45 |

| | |
|---|---|
| Pansy earrings | 50-70 |
| Blue bow | 30-50 |
| Violet pin | 40-60 |
| Circle pin | 25-50 |
| Earrings, sterling | 45-60 |
| Bar pin | 25-50 |
| p-122. Six Eisenberg pins | 450-550 each |
| Egyptian pin | 500-up |
| p-123.   Floral brooch, blue | 475-500 |
| Floral brooch, red | 400-450 |
| p-124. Floral spray pin | 325-375 |
| Bonsai pin | 275-325 |
| Flowers pin, Carnegie | 295-350 |
| Blossom pin | 325-375 |
| p-125. Floral spray | 400-450 |
| Blossom | 325-375 |
| p-126. Blue drop pin | 1000-1100 |
| Yellow flower pin | 650-725 |
| Pink bouquet pin | 1200-1250 |
| Basket of flowers pin | 1200-1250 |
| Green plant pin | 675-725 |
| Yellow bouquet pin | 650-700 |
| Yellow and rhine-stones pin | 750-800 |
| Blue with leaves pin | 850-900 |
| Plastic stones and chain pin | 250-300 |
| Oval pin | 500-550 |
| Bouquet pin | 1100-1200 |
| p-127. Bracelet | 395-450 |
| Pin and earrings | 450-500 |
| Pink plastic pin | 70-125 |
| Gold washed pin | 325-400 |
| p-128. Iridescent pin | 175-200 |
| Sterling and pink pin | 250-325 |
| Bouquet pin | 85-110 |
| Pin and earrings, pink | 125-175 |
| Thistle pin and earrings | 125-175 |
| p-129. Bouquet pin | 95-125 |
| Pink trembling pin | 125-150 |
| Trembling set | 245-300 |
| Round pin | 150-225 |
| Three flowers pin | 75-140 |
| p-130. Shell pin | 60-85 |
| Butterfly stick pin | 75-120 |
| Bouquet pin | 125-150 |
| Wheat sheafs pin | 45-75 |
| Plastic beads pin | 75-95 |
| p-131. Shells pin | 450-500 |
| Plastic beads pin | 175-250 |
| p-132. Blue glass pin | 425-470 |
| Bouquet pin | 300-375 |
| Brass and silver pin | 90-125 |
| p-133. Tree pin | 250-275 |
| Blossom pin | 75-130 |
| Gold pin, Eisenberg | 225-295 |
| Man and Cornucopia pin | 250-325 |
| p-134. Pin and earrings | 75-100 |
| Art Deco pin | 2000-2100 |
| p-135. Clip, Eisenberg | 350-400 |
| Sterling fan clip | 275-300 |

| | |
|---|---|
| Large round clip | 250-300 |
| Small round clip | 225-275 |
| Double clip brooch | 110-130 |
| Pin by Kramer | 75-100 |
| Art Deco pin | 375-400 |
| p-136. Single clip | 400-450 |
| Pair of clips | 475-500 |
| Fountain pin | 400-450 |
| Triangular pin | 95-150 |
| Bar pin | 85-110 |
| p-137. Clock hands pin | 300-350 |
| Jabot pin | 200-225 |
| Eisenbert clip | 325-375 |
| Colored glass clip | 95-120 |
| p-138. Clip with tassels | 300-350 |
| Ring | 150-200 |
| Pair of clips | 300-350 |
| Pierced fan clip | 250-275 |
| Pin by Reja | 300-325 |
| Pin by Beal-Ron | 75-120 |
| p-139. Colored glass pin | 65-75 |
| Round pin | 60-85 |
| François pin | 50-95 |
| Art pin | 50-95 |
| p-140. Four pins | 300-375 each |
| Pin and earrings | 375-400 |
| Three circles pin | 45-75 |
| Brown pin | 50-80 |
| Triangular pin | 90-135 |
| p-141. Trifari pin | 325-350 |
| Schreiner pin | 100-140 |
| Black enamel pin | 75-100 |
| Di Nicola pin | 325-350 |
| p-142. Heart and cupid pin | 295-325 |
| Earrings | 295-325 |
| Heart and arrow pin | 250-300 |
| Face pin | 1000-1200 |
| Red and clear stone pin | 400-450 |
| Necklace | 900-1050 |
| Light blue heart pin | 650-700 |
| Green heart pin | 475-550 |
| Triple hearts pin | 675-725 |
| Dark blue heart pin | 600-625 |
| Red and white heart pin | 650-700 |
| p-143. Square pin | 700-750 |
| Crescent pin | 600-650 |
| Oval pin | 700-750 |
| Bow pin | 550-600 |
| Brown stones pin | 650-700 |
| Light blue stone pin | 700-725 |
| Green stone pin | 700-725 |
| Pink and green stone pin | 700-725 |
| p-144. Four bow pins | 425-475 each |
| Vogue pin | 225-275 |
| Chanel pin, base metal | 125-150 |
| Eisenberg pin | 650-700 |
| p-145. Rhinestone and central pearl pin | 225-250 |
| Bow pin | 225-250 |
| Circle pin | 125-175 |
| Ribbon pin | 125-175 |
| Cross-shaped pin | 225-250 |

| | |
|---|---|
| Crystal bow pin | 450-500 |
| p-146. Sterling bow pin | 300-350 |
| Pearl and rhinestone pin | 350-375 |
| Bow pin | 300-350 |
| Vendome pin | 275-300 |
| Blue bow pin | 400-450 |
| Danecraft pin | 250-275 |
| Circle pin | 200-250 |
| p-147. Tanger star pin | 65-85 |
| Schiaparelli star pin | 75-100 |
| Medallions | 150-225 each |
| p-148. Green earrings | 95-150 |
| Paste and pearl earrings | 75-140 |
| French earrings | 400-500 |
| Austrian pin | 95-140 |
| Necklace | 200-250 |
| p-149. Clip earrings | 45-75 |
| Dangle earrings | 75-100 |
| French earrings | 125-200 |
| Fish earrings | 95-160 |
| p-150. Papier Mache earrings | 110-145 |
| Openwork earrings | 200-250 |
| Markasite earrings | 120-170 |
| Cameo earrings | 150-195 |
| p-151. French earrings | 175-195 |
| German earrings | 125-160 |
| Green drop earrings | 150-175 |
| Red drop earrings | 150-185 |
| p-152. Pearl earrings | 200-240 |
| Pink earrings | 70-95 |
| Red ear clips | 140-195 |
| Silver clip earrings | 120-150 |
| Brown earrings | 55-75 |
| p-153. Purple earrings | 75-100 |
| Pin and earrings | 60-85 |
| Mazer earrings | 55-75 |
| Polcini earrings | 50-75 |
| p-154. Bar pin | 75-95 |
| Large crystal drop earrings | 125-175 |
| Single crystal earrings | 100-130 |
| Blue earrings | 100-125 |
| Teardrop and rectangle earrings | 100-125 |
| Small crystal drop earrings | 125-150 |
| Floral and drop earrings | 150-200 |
| Pin and earrings, green | 50-75 |
| Pin and earrings, purple | 50-75 |
| Pin and earrings, amber | 50-75 |
| Pearl drop earrings | 85-100 |
| Red stone earrings | 100-130 |
| p-155. Ivory face earrings | 50-70 |
| Aqua stone earrings | 150-175 |
| Enamel shoe earrings | 50-80 |
| Mazer earrings | 50-80 |
| Coral earrings | 95-120 |
| Pin and earrings | 100-125 |

p-156. Hoop earrings        225-275
   Pearl drop earrings      225-275
   Lane earrings            300-up
   Ear covers               50-75
p-157. (above) Aqua
   earrings                 125-150
   Ram's head earrings 95-120
   Orange pavé
   earrings                 125-150
   Green enamel
   earrings                 100-125
   Rhinestone and
   green earrings           100-125
   (below) Red, white
   and blue earrings        100-125
   Pink and blue
   dangle earrings          225-295
   Green drop earrings 125-170
   Red and green
   earrings                 95-120
   Red and white
   earrings                 100-140
   Butterfly earrings       90-125
   Blue drop earrings       100-125
   Red drop earrings        125-150
   Crescent earrings        125-140
   Bow drop earrings        125-140
p-158. Earrings            50-65 each
   Pearl necklace with
   enameled pendant 65-90
   Pearl necklace and
   bracelet with
   pendant                  65-90
   String of pearls
   necklace                 60-85
p-159. Large pearl
   earrings                 125-160
   Red earrings             140-175
   Gold nest earrings       120-150
   Plastic and pearl
   earrings                 125-150
   Black circle earrings 160-180
   Square earrings          150-170
   Black drop earrings      120-170
p-160. Black and white
   pin                      100-120
   Red star earrings        90-125
   Interwoven enamel
   ear clips                100-125
   Pearl drop earrings      140-175
   Red and white hoop
   earrings                 100-140
   Gold and pearl hoop
   earrings                 90-125
   Heart earrings           100-140
   Bull's eye earrings      90-120
   Checkerboard
   earrings                 90-120
   Square earrings          125-175